The Second Chance

The Second Chance

Ralph Harper

TRINITY PRESS INTERNATIONAL
Valley Forge, Pennsylvania

First Edition 1993
Trinity Press International
P.O. Box 851
Valley Forge, PA 19482-0851

Cover Design by Jim Gerhard

Library of Congress Cataloging-in-Publication Data

Harper, Ralph,
    The second chance / Ralph Harper. — 1st ed.
        p.   cm.
    Includes bibliographical references.
    ISBN 1-56338-059-5:
    1. Harper, Ralph.   2. Episcopal Church—Clergy—
Bibliography.   3. Anglican Communion—United States—Clergy—
Bibliography.   I. Title.
BX5995.H34A3   1993
283′.092—dc20
[B]   93-1237
                                                                      CIP

Printed in the United States of America.
93 94 95 96 97 98   6 5 4 3 2 1

Preface

This book began as an attempt to uncover the hidden assumptions of my life. Along the way it turned into something else, as I was forced to acknowledge elements of a spirituality that is existential rather than theological. So what began as a spiritual autobiography ended with the discovery of elements of a new kind of spirituality, one arising from experience instead of tradition.

Until now I have always been wary of using such words as *spirit* and *spirituality*. Although I am only too aware of the freight these words bear, I find I have no better words to say what I mean.

I know that personal narrative, whether reflective or lyrical, can be dismissed as merely personal. I hope that because it is personal, my narrative will remind others of what sometimes goes on at the edge of their minds as well.

Some of what I say here touches on the subliminal, and that is not easy to write about. I have already tried in *On Presence*. But just as there are two kinds of presence, subliminal and constant on the one hand, and open and occasional on the other, so I believe the shape of a secret self, sometimes shadowy, sometimes quite distinct, underlies and gives character to both kinds of presence. Together, presence and the secret self are the principal features of a spirituality that reaches out to the mystery of all things.

The Second Chance

They are gone now
the ones he saw
through the bars
coming up the ferry ramp
from the fog-bound harbor
carrying their secrets with them

In the winter of my seventy-sixth year I decided suddenly to
go back to Oxford for a weekend after an absence of fifty-
two years. I thought that by returning to the place where
the course of my life was set I might be able to start all over.
What I have to say about this probably cannot interest anyone who is satisfied with his or her life. For my story is
about a person who once thought he knew himself well and
came to find out he did not.

The fact is I feel less certain about myself at the very
time that I recognize that I have done almost everything I
wanted to do. I have come to see that for much of my life I
have been holding myself in, not only saying less than I
know, but thinking less than I ought to know. I have held
myself in so long that by now I do not always know what is
often clearer to others than to myself.

It is ironic that anyone who has spent his professional
life thinking about the interior life should be unclear about
his own. But I have found, almost too late, that it is possi-

ble to be so blind to oneself that one can miss what is most characteristic. I don't think I have tried to hide myself from myself, but it seems that in hiding myself from others I have come to take myself for granted, and as a result have not always seen myself as I really am.

I suppose everyone has secrets, large or small. I have never known anyone who did not. And because even trivial secrets about oneself can be embarrassing, many are inclined to pretend that they are open books. I am not concerned about trivial secrets, even embarrassing ones, only the more elusive basic elements of the person I really am.

Some of us protect ourselves by pretending that we are better than we know we are. Some of us figure that we will be admired if we praise ourselves enough. Pretending is an important part of anyone's strategy for self-protection. Who has not done his share of pretending to prop up his self-esteem a little? It is normal to hide uncomfortable truths from ourselves as well as from others. No one can afford to be fully known.

I wrote a book about spy stories because I was fascinated by what one has to go through to hide what he really is. I knew from observing real people, as well as characters in novels, what it is like to lead a double life, and to be forced to juggle different personalities, even—at times—two sets of facts. I was fascinated by the strain of slipping in and out of character. "Will my mask slip?"

It only takes an imaginative writer like Sherwood Anderson to remind us that behind the closed doors and windows of row upon row of homes in towns all over America, in the Midwest, in New England, and the South, are secrets, "grotesques"[1] innumerable. Across a quiet street on a summer night a woman screams hysterically, or a man sobs uncontrollably and frightens a child who has brought him flowers from his church, or a thin little man comes to one's door one night and cries, "But I am still a priest!" or the brilliant brother of the girl one has just taken to the beach unaccountably kills himself. Who knows what goes on behind the buttoned-up façades of empty streets?

Most people would not readily admit to leading a double life, to having a secret self. Indeed, most people would prefer not to admit having any secrets that make them vulnerable. There are times when, if we knew some things about others that are kept hidden, we would judge them quite differently. Politicians especially live in perpetual fear of exposure. But who knows how many of the rest of us would crumble if everything were known? And yet, how can any of us be understood, how can we understand ourselves, if portions of our lives are forever suppressed? Of course, there are secret selves in all of us, secret to others, but secret also to ourselves. But as time goes by, what might seem scandalous may come to seem trivial. Then what for a time had looked like a secret self turns out to be just a life that has some secrets.

Confiding in others may release the self, at least temporarily. We sometimes look to others for absolution, but mainly we look for enough understanding to ease the essential loneliness that is a part of living. What is confided is not as important as the motive for confiding. In truth, it is terribly difficult to share ourselves with anyone else, much harder for some than for others. Because so much is unfinished, confidential exposure may have the unwanted effect of inhibiting us further. So some confidences lead to disillusion, and other confidences make us feel we are empty and worthless.

Psychiatrists despair when their patients resist giving up some final piece of themselves. Sometimes people hold even a trivial secret in reserve as proof that they are not pawns of anyone else, including the doctors they are paying to assist in their liberation. We keep secrets to prove that we are different. In the end it is not by any means easy to tell the difference between secrets and a secret self.

If we really had a secret self, something solid and compact that is partly secret even to ourselves, we should not need little secrets to prove we are not like other people. But it is more difficult to become aware of having a secret self: something achieved, not something inherited. And it is all the more difficult to identify any special inner dynamic that separates each of us from others, a pattern of individuation.

I believe that even the faintest outline of such a self is likely to be misty, also likely to suggest instability. Now we see it, now we don't, because now it is this, and now it is that. One feature after another comes into the open for a while, and then fades, the whole self eluding comprehension.

Nothing thought
that must be hidden
Nothing hidden
that cannot be said
Nothing said
that will not be remembered
That is how it has been
and that is how it will be

I should be quite willing to reveal my secret self, if I knew what it is. That is, I think I would. I do not think there could be anything embarrassing about it that I could not face. But if I am not sure of what my self is, it is not easy to imagine that anything would be lost were it disclosed. Judging by what I usually think of confidential disclosures, my secret self might turn out to be rather uninteresting, and even abstract.

Is *self* just a word we use conventionally to express the complexity of our existence, our individuality, our personality, our character? Is there no nub, no knot, no thing either hard or jellyish inside? Do we even have a right to speak of self as one, as single? Could there not, indeed, are there not all too often many selves, a kaleidoscope of selves, some on the surface, some deep inside, succeeding, overlapping, like masks? Stendhal liked asking, "Do I really know myself? It is this that sometimes saddens me in the middle of the night, when I brood over it."

But when I say "secret self," I have in mind a few central obsessions that shape me even when I am not thinking about them. Augustine, who said, "Man is a great deep," also said, "I cannot totally grasp all that I am. There is something of man that the very spirit of man that is in him does not know. A man is for the most part unknown even to himself." I think he was right.

Like many others I have taken myself for granted, just because I have lived with myself so long. One can become foolishly proud of what one sees as personal continuity. What a shock to suspect that self-assurance may just be a cover for ignorance, and an excuse not to change. Is there not often someone quite small and scared inside? We are sometimes tempted to think of other people as having no self at all. Some may, it is true, have underdeveloped or retarded selves. Others are so mixed up about their identities that they know they do not know themselves. There is always something else that might be uncovered, something that would make a difference between functional and purposeful living.

Would it make it any easier if I were to stop saying "secret self" and just say "elusive self"? It might let me evade the question of whether I am speaking of a permanent self. I should only be saying that whoever I am, I am difficult to put in words. I should then be shifting from a kind of personal metaphysics to epistemology. It is what philosophers do all the time. It makes thinking easier.

I shall not do this because I know too much about myself that makes it impossible to evade questions about the nature of the self. The self may be elusive, but it is not unknowable, just extremely hard to talk about.

He thought he could not tell
a story
even though he spent his time
reading stories
in the end
he wanted nothing else
than to tell himself
the story of his life

This is a delicate matter. The self is not only tempted to be devious, sometimes with good intentions, but keeps eluding one no matter how hard one tries to be honest. What is nearer self than self, and what is farther away from comprehension? Could not a reason for the elusiveness be that while we look for what is hidden, the self just ticks away like a clock, a little noisily? It never goes away, and it seldom stands at attention for long.

Does it make a difference whether the self is secret or whether it is just elusive? To those who do not have much experience with introspection the distinction may seem trivial. But it is by no means a waste of time to admit that you are no longer sure you know yourself as well as you thought.

To see the self as elusive, constantly out of reach, is to see that human beings are labyrinthine. But it is out of such labyrinths that something new can appear. When Proust said that the experience of the self is the only true experience, he was implying that it is a model for all experience. If we can know ourselves, we should be able to know anything else also without barriers. One kind of presence is not dissimilar to others. We can carry over into one kind of experience the immediacy or the separateness of others. This is the reason why novelists—for example, Proust—feel that it is easier to write about the self by writing about someone else, a fictional self, an "other self," to use Rilke's words.

Most of the time, in desperation, we peel away slivers of ourselves, until at last we think we have found a spare self or two to show others. The other self that eludes is sometimes the very lie we have been telling about ourselves. Unusually sensitive persons—Kierkegaard and Kafka, let us say—tempt us to believe, as they themselves did, that there is a self-isolated self behind some door with a jammed lock or a bottomless fear. Then we would look no further. But I refuse to believe that the mask or the lie is the last word. At the very least, I think it is possible to try not to deceive ourselves. Proust said that we lack the sense of our own visibility, not because we are perverse but because we are blinded by many other truths that have little to do with us.

There is a difference between one who has begun to wonder what he can know about himself and one who knows quite well that there is something consistent and permanent about his personality. The difference may not matter in the end, if it has the effect of maintaining equilibrium. It is an achievement to know what one's secret self is: it is more of an achievement to have one at all. Not everyone does, it seems.

What enables any of us to get beyond what we have taken for granted? I believe that a major change in life is likely to be preceded by some crisis so complete that the resources of the old self cannot handle it. Then the choice lies between being saved or foundering. To be saved one would, as it were, have to go into reverse, changing one's view of many things. No real transformation is going to take place without a profound shake-up. Indeed, self-knowledge by itself will not be enough to loosen the roots of entrenched solitude. If the self is to continue to grow, it has to die a little first, or at least be cauterized. I do not see how this can happen in isolation from others. We need someone else to confirm what is happening. Only then can enough healing of the wound to self-esteem make it safe for us to face an uncertain future.

7

Once there was a child
in a dark blue coat
blue hat and white socks
walking down a sandy road
with pail and shovel
Now there is an old man
with pen and pad
making verses

There is more than one way to feel one's life is right. The usual way is to imagine things we want to do and, when we do them, say we are successful. The trouble comes when we succeed and then are not satisfied. Somehow we have been cheated.

We have an instinct for what would make us feel justified that has little to do with accepted values, and we are bewildered when we compare this instinct with the goals of other people. Unless we learn to separate our goals from others', we risk ultimate discouragement. It is bad enough to fail in the eyes of others, but much worse to fail when we compare our own instincts to others' easy certainties. And it is much worse to feel uncertain about what we really should be up to.

It is impossible not to live to some degree in terms that civilized people have fought over. But if we are to have anything remotely like defensible self-confidence, we must try to be like those whose inner destiny did not depend exclusively on received values. For them a conflict must also have taken place between inner and outer. But they knew their minds in the end and fought for what they believed in.

Self-confidence is not necessarily dependent on a secret self. In fact, the more one suspects he has a secret self, the less confident he may become that outward success means much. Not that it matters what other people think: it is what I myself think I have not done that really matters.

What we do know is that if the outer life fails, we at least might still have a secret self to fall back on, a reserve to depend on when all else fails. It may be only then that some people become aware of having a secret self however faint. Most of the serious disappointments in life, however, have nothing much to do with a secret self, which usually remains untouched.

I am not thinking here about autonomy. The most independent persons can experience devastating failure. If a person puts all his hopes on attaining goals that make sense to other people, and has nothing of his own to work for, he can be destroyed when he thinks he has fallen below their standards. When what we do is mainly what other people approve of, the shape of any secret self within will remain undetected. And yet a secret self is not a luxury: it is a bedrock.

Somewhere
under the surface
I don't know
how far
there is a truth
that if known
would make all the difference

It is possible that everyone has a secret self and that many do not find it, or find it too late. But I do not know whether this is true. I know only myself, and yet I hope that what I have to say may stir some interest in others who do not have the words yet to describe what they feel.

Should we not hope to bring the hidden self, if we have one, out into the open? Is there any point in keeping it hidden? The sooner it is out the better, but only when we know enough about it not to fear its being squashed by the misunderstandings of other people.

When I speak of my secret self, I am thinking of a few underlying certainties that give me a defining sense of who I am. The first is my appreciation of the shortness of time to live, and the urgency that goes with this. The second is my aloneness, and the third a persistent longing to complete myself in some undefined way.

Beyond these three interior thoughts about myself is my conviction, formed by experience and observation, that I will not be completed by my own agency. At some critical point my completion will depend on unexpected events or unexpected encounters with other people.

These are existential elements of my soul, so to speak, and can, I believe, be experienced by others.

Why do I then stress the secrecy of the self, since I have already revealed how much I understand about myself? The answer is that I did not see these things clearly and together until very recently, and I suspect that others will similarly not understand themselves easily either. Until now I have held the four elements of my understanding of myself uncollated inside my mind, and spoken and written about them only in the course of writing about other people's ideas.

Spiralling bands
of black and white
overlapping bands
of gold and white
nature and artifice
quill and ring
flesh and spirit
together as one
ecstasy into repose

When I was still an undergraduate at Harvard and trying to write like a philosopher, I wrote a little book called *Alien*

Spears[2] that provoked an accomplished philosopher to say that I already had a poetic imagination and a powerful dialectical skill. I liked that, of course. But it was at the time only a goal to strive for, not one already attained. I had begun to see my own mind in terms of a Kierkegaardian polarity of aesthetic and dialectic. In more ordinary words, it was a polarity of reflection and imagination, philosophy and poetry.

It was quite some time before I realized the inhibiting power philosophy was having over my imagination. For a long time I did not know how to free myself from the abstractness I said I despised in others more capable than I. And yet I kept reading both philosophy and poetry. I even wrote a little of the latter, and more of the former, keeping the two at arms' length from each other. I was not ignorant of the legitimate claims of each and fantasized that one day I might have vision and skill enough to combine them.

This was one reason why I never became the disciple of any of the philosophers or theologians I read. Also, I found I could not agree completely with any of those I admired. There was always some place where I had to turn away. And not in Kierkegaard, least of all in Heidegger, could I find a perfect marriage between mind and imagination. Only in Augustine's *Confessions* did I find such a model.

So I arranged my own ideas and images within the proven context of minds other than my own, and still tried to keep myself at a little distance. A theologian I had not met once wrote to persuade me to stop using the word *existential* to describe what I was doing. He said that I had something of my own to say. But I knew I was not ready, and I likened myself to the unsuccessful writer in Henry James's story "The Next Time," who kept hoping that each new novel would break through into financial success. None did. Each was an exquisite failure. I felt that like him I may have become too sophisticated.

He learned to speak
so clearly in other people's tongues
it is no wonder
he could not hear himself
at all

I now see that I have something in common with the narrator of Proust's last novel who imagines himself as an old man tottering on a mountain of accumulated memories. It is time, I thought, to level my own mountain of borrowed wisdom. I ought to try to put aside much of what I have read and start all over. And yet had I been unaffected by fifty years of exposure to the thoughts of others? Would not my self be impoverished if suddenly deprived of their hard-won insights?

As a teacher I had tried to identify the motifs that could be heard in the songs and voices of the novelists, poets, and philosophers we discussed in class. I wanted to be, I tried hard to be, scrupulous in interpreting them. I hoped that if they could listen in, they would recognize themselves in what we said.

Sometimes I speculated on how I would have behaved had I been put in a Nazi concentration camp. What good would all my reading do? Or my books? Where would I get strength to go on, without losing my integrity? I hardly dared try to answer. For secure as my life had been, I knew enough about the demoralizing effects of pressure, provocation, and fatigue, let alone torture and the sight of others' suffering. Could it be that my integrity might in any way be supported by knowing that I had a secret self that no one could take away from me?

For most of my life I had firmly held that the accumulated wisdom earned by study and reflection had formed an individuality that should be identifiable to others, and, what's more, dependable. I knew that some who knew me well did not totally share my self-mistrust. Perhaps they thought that I had inner resources that I myself was ignorant of.

> *Perhaps we remember*
> *so much*
> *so that somehow*
> *sometime*
> *we might improve*
> *upon our beginning*

When I revisited Oxford, I had such thoughts in mind. I was tempted to think that I had a chance to start all over, and by trying to exorcise self-mistrust see my final course. I imagined, somewhat dramatically, that when I saw the ancient colleges again, I should be able quite easily to strengthen my resolve. I supposed that I might count on my return to direct both mind and imagination for one last lap.

To walk around the colleges is like walking through a stone maze, façades blind even when not windowless. After one day of walking the narrow lanes, I began to feel drained of everything my mind had brought with it from America. It was as if something or someone had very quietly removed my old identity, so that I might be ready for a new life.

I was staying once more at Campion Hall where I had lived for two years as a graduate student. Some reluctance to retrace my life at first kept me from walking around Christ Church Meadow, which was only a little distance from Campion Hall. And even when, after two days, I felt like leaving the confined streets between the colleges, I chose for my first stroll Addison's Walk at Magdalen. When I was a graduate student I seldom walked there, preferring Christ Church Meadow because it was nearer Campion Hall and was bounded by both the Thames and the Cherwell.

But on my third day back I returned to the Meadow. It was as if I had not seen it before, the paths wider and longer, and there were now young women jogging and women's eights on the river.

By that time I had dined at both Keble and Campion, an honored old boy. I had had lunch with Isaiah Berlin at Old Souls and with F. W. Dillistone at Oriel. I had called on my old theology tutor, Harry Carpenter, now retired Bishop of Oxford. And two old friends came back to see me: Frank Prince, poet, and our mutual friend, Albert Hourani, historian of the Arab peoples. Once again I was with people with whom I could talk without inhibition. Had I all along known that this was why I had wanted to return?

On the afternoon of my last day, a new friend, the present Master of Campion Hall, Father Joseph Munitiz, accompanied me up the river to Port Meadow where I used to walk and bathe, to Binsey, familiar to readers of Hopkins's poems. When we came to Binsey in a drizzle and entered the tiny church, the curate in cassock was about to ring the bell for Evensong. At that moment I felt that he was ringing the bell for my own future.

On our way back into the city we peered through the locked glass door of St. Barnabas, the ritualistic church known to those who read Oxford novels. Then I went off by myself to Evensong at Christ Church Cathedral. I had never attended Evensong there before. My one memory of the cathedral was hearing Vaughan Williams' "Lark Ascending," with violin and organ, one late afternoon during the war.

Between space and silence
there is nothing
and in most speech
and in most silence
there is also nothing

I have never taken much interest in space travel. And yet in sleep I have had upsetting nightmares of flying through the skies and across oceans, sometimes back to Oxford. In some of these dreams I was in an airplane; in others I was obliged to cling precariously to an open rocket ship, suffering frightfully from vertigo and dread of death.

In my waking moments I have always assumed that life is meant to be a voyage from the onset of consciousness to a state of mind where I should at last be able to match all important questions with answers. I never supposed that after reading many books I could ever turn my back on their assembled wisdom.

In the West, classical and Christian metaphors for the passage through life are similar. The voyage in both cases ends in death, but also ends with some assurance that life has been worth living and can be understood. Both Homeric and Augustinian patterns for the voyage promise a return to the simplicity of the beginning.

Life is not an endless voyage, we all know that, even when, as in the case of Odysseus, it threatens to be. His voyage had been around an inland sea, and he sailed from shore to shore, guided by a conviction that he would know his home when he got there. Augustine, too, felt that the course of his life, his inner life, could be understood as a return to an end that was implicit in his beginning.

But in my dream of hurtling through space there was to be no return to earth, and no homecoming, only a stomach-churning flight and near certainty of a final crash. Some part of my mind held out hope that at best the flight might not end, and I could go on living. That I did not have these nightmares until I was past seventy suggested that contrary to my paradigms I was being forced by a sense of reality to admit the possibility that the longing I was accustomed to think of as nostalgia had no meaning whatsoever.

How could I look for wisdom and at the end of life conclude that all I had reflected on was largely irrelevant to me? The least one should be able to say is that one has fought the good fight. To me that had always meant, in part, reflecting on the wisdom of the great. And now I was discovering that that had left me less satisfaction than I had counted on. I seemed to have come to a standstill.

This then was the reason why I had to return to Oxford. I said to myself, "If you go back to that port of departure, you may find the rules of the voyage posted somewhere, rules you missed when you were there as a young man." I had supposed that I had the right ticket for the long voyage, and had now discovered that it only permitted me to stand on deck, without seat or shelter from the wind and spray. No sooner had the ship left port than I found there was no berth for me. I spent many years trying to earn the extra ticket for a berth inside, only to be ejected from cabins again and again—an experience I have had in the Aegean. When, after years, I seemed to have found a cabin and a berth just for me, I also found that I would not be allowed to sleep. The more I clung to my right to use a cabin and berth, the more insecure I felt about the destination of the ship. Finally I began to fear that there was no destination at all, just an endless voyage.

The longer I stayed on the ship, the more tired I became. At last I jumped ship and began to drown. At this point in life I woke up, realizing that I had had the wrong metaphor for life. I had been taken in by received wisdom, Homeric and Augustinian. Perhaps I had wanted to be deceived. For who does not prefer to think that truth is out there somewhere, accessible, waiting for us to find and make our own?

He was waiting
for the silence
and the speech
that would fill up
the hollow places
from top to bottom

Proust said that as one grows older, quiet more and more surrounds one. When I placed this alongside Kafka's K's enormous fatigue, I had two metaphors close to my own state. But these too gave me no hope. I seemed to have learned nothing that might save me, in all my fifty years of reading, teaching, preaching, and writing. I had joined all the rest who mislead earnest seekers like myself. I had at best distracted myself so that I could keep the worst fears under control. The dreams of rocketing through space signified a ruthlessly controlled dread that I might have to make it alone, with no sure guide or companion. This had been the initial dread of my childhood.

Why had it taken so long to see that in spite of the intellectual satisfaction of observing similarities between my mind and those of the famous, I would never be able to see anything important that they had not seen before me? The more assiduously I worked through their books, the more tired I became. I found myself repeating what the brightest and best had already said.

I had been assuming that there are only so many truths and that I had time to find them. Even though I knew there is not enough time for everyone else, I wanted to believe there would be time enough for me. The longer I lived, the more I believed that time was on my side. How disillusioning to suspect suddenly that time had not been on my side, and that whatever gifts I had been given, wisdom was not one of them. Then I, too, began to feel the quiet settling around me.

I had obviously been mistaken about what ultimately satisfies. Had I wasted my life learning the good models? Name them, I had read them all; worse, I had written about them; worse still, I had tried to convince others to believe in them. I had not convinced myself. And so I began to withdraw from received wisdom. Even before this I had with regret laid aside religious interpretations that seemed to reflect wishful thinking rather than first-hand observation.

No longer tempted to play with packaged truth, I was even less tempted to retreat to any kind of doctrinaire skepticism. Disillusionment with myself was not accompanied by denial of things that I was convinced were either real or good. Nor should anyone try now to tell me what I had not experienced myself. Nevertheless, I had to admit that I had become a traveler with no plausible itinerary.

I think most of us would like to be able to reject endlessness, as a child does when he wonders where the sky goes. I still hoped that I was being given more time, already longer than my parents had had, to be saved from feeling that I was no better off at the end than at the beginning. I did not think I could get any satisfaction out of saying, "At least I know what I do not know." Even Socrates knew more than he pretended. And I was not one who could get satisfaction out of the struggle alone. My mind, like most people's, tends to look for conclusions, and to want to stay with them. Was there to be no rest? Could I live with the indeterminate? Did I have a choice? Had my empirical honesty brought me to this?

That winter day
in Thailand
when he sat alone
in the heat
and the stillness
by a flowing river
idly watching villagers
being ferried from shore to shore
while the cotton weavers' looms
clicked and clacked behind him
and he was at peace

Several years ago, while visiting my older son in Thailand, on my return home I experienced unusual disorientation, not, I think, ascribable just to jet lag. For some days I felt I belonged nowhere. And I fancied that if I could find a way to return to Bangkok, I might recover the self that was lost.

One night I dreamed that someone was knocking on the door of our hotel room in Chiang Mai. When I opened the door, I saw a woman I had never seen before. That was the dream. Much later it occurred to me that my disorientation after coming home may have lasted so long because I had had to leave that dream unfinished.

Only now do I recall that this dream fragment was not unlike my state of mind when I was a student at Oxford and day after day there and when on vacation in Fribourg, Florence, and Innsbruck, I would say my prayers before images of the Blessed Virgin Mary. The difference was that in the dream in Chiang Mai she, or someone, had at last come to me.

Recently I came across a line in one of my books that speaks to this. "I was looking for you all the time before I knew you existed."[3] I had wanted to suggest that there is a similar pattern of longing in both religious and sexual love.

Even when I wrote that sentence, I knew that both Augustine and John of the Cross would have seen it that way. Perhaps unconsciously I was echoing what I had read. I had tried so hard to see life as they did, and failed.

Kneeling before images of the Blessed Virgin, like Henry Adams, I prayed that in her loving mercy she might take and hold me. Now, of course, I can see the sexual as well as spiritual aspects of my fervor. I do not think I ever believed that the Queen of Heaven was real, like women I could see in the streets. I could not touch her, although I would have had I been able. I wanted most of all to be accepted as I was, without being ridiculed. Neither she nor the Blessed Sacrament on the altar of churches ever became a satisfying substitute for the reality beyond the doors of the churches I entered. Once out in the fresh air, the prayer, the dream, the mystery evaporated, and I was alone once more.

It has taken a long time to understand what my longing was up to. You might say it was only a matter of time before I would wake up. There have been times when I wished I had not woken up. For others I know the dream has gone on, and I watch them from a distance, with the sympathy of one who once was where they are.

He knew he was in the South
when he heard the fish pedlar
singing in the street
outside his shuttered bedroom
and heard the trolley bell
lurching round the corner
and breathed the fragrance
of the garden beds below

Before I left Oxford in 1940, I found another way to express the polarity of aesthetic and dialectic. Still searching for some way to put together my own contradictions, I found the words *radiance* and *intricacy*. They seemed to edge me closer to what I saw outside as well as inside my mind.

By this time I had read even more poetry and fiction, more theology and more philosophy. I had seen more art and architecture. I had been exposed to the beauties of Italy and Switzerland as well as England and New England. Without knowing it then, I was preparing my sensibilities for a lifelong love of the Greek islands. From that time I became addicted to the sensuousness of the physical world. And it was in Greece that I understood clearly for the first time that my religious sentiments could not live outside the walls of churches. I knew that if I were ever to pray again, I should have to take that into account. In other words, I stopped confusing faith with sentiment.

Much later I came to understand that I had been pre-pared for this state of mind since childhood, when my mother took me back to her old home in Charleston, South Carolina every spring. On leaving the train station my senses were drowned in the sounds and scents of a south-ern street. The contrast between the soundless, scentless snowbound New England and Charleston in the spring set its mark on me for the rest of my life.

I was thus introduced to the radiance of the world long before I learned anything about the intricacy of the mind. I would need the rest of a long schooling to learn that intri-cacy only too thoroughly. The disciplines of an intellectual life are wonderful in themselves, but they sometimes stunt the growth of sensuousness.

I had also yet to learn another lesson, that there are people who are radiant. When I met such people at Oxford, intellectuals, artists, I confused the radiance of their person-alities with the shining intricacy of their minds. Father Mar-tin D'Arcy and David Jones come to mind. I wanted to be like them, and succeeded to the degree that I became too subtle for my own good.

When I returned to Oxford, Father D'Arcy and David Jones were long gone. But I met Isaiah Berlin again, and he told me of a crucial conversation he once had with a Harvard philosopher, Henry Sheffer, who had persuaded him that while original insights can be had by able people, there is really no progress possible in philosophy because we cannot add anything to what minds such as Plato, Aristotle, or Kant have said. Their ideas are not obsolete, like some scientific ideas; they have a life of their own and we do not advance beyond them.[4]

I know that it is possible to see the world as a Platonist or an Aristotelian or a Kantian. But I also know from my own studies of the existentialists that each of the men I have spent so much time reading—Barth, Buber, Marcel, Jaspers, Heidegger—did not think in a vacuum. They stood on the shoulders of others, including Plato, Aristotle, and Kant, and especially on the shoulders of Nietzsche, Kierkegaard, Pascal, and Augustine. Existential thinking, at least, has been cumulative.

One thing I have found difficult to accept is that so many of my contemporaries have been unwilling to include existential themes in their thinking. These are the themes of the interior life that should be familiar to all of us. Kierkegaard was the first to protest against this exclusion. I like to remember Camus's dictum, "Nothing is true that forces one to exclude." Academic philosophy in the present century has been impoverished by exclusion.

Camus also said that to do philosophy one should write novels. I say, if you cannot do that, at least try to use their insights, especially the insights of Dostoevsky, Proust, and Kafka. They offer an experiential corrective to hyperanalysis. Tillich suggested another corrective when he said somewhere that the study of the mystics would turn out to be a good source for such insights, too. I tapped that source even before I had heard of Tillich.

I know as well as anyone that there is little that any of us can say that has not already been said. Camus, again, said that it takes ten years to have one or two simple ideas of one's own. He got it about right, except that I would add that we are lucky if we do as well. But it is possible, as the existentialists have shown. Most of us scarcely go beyond underlining and rearranging the thoughts of others. Even that can amount to standing on their shoulders, and by doing so we can make a little progress in philosophy. My own themes have been solitude, disquietude, nostalgia, and presence.

When we try to be scrupulous, we aim to find the individual voice in the books we are reading. We can save ourselves from both imitation and idolatry by the personal intensity with which we seek what is true. It is passion that is the telltale sign of individual conviction—where there is conviction and not just empty intensity—especially when accompanied by respect for the differences between us.

Recently I noticed that for all that I have read and remembered, I am often slow to see what is important. It sometimes takes an observation of someone else to make my own ideas clear to me.

Perhaps delays in seeing things that should be obvious happen because we spend so much time on the ideas of others and neglect our own. It is much easier to deal with ideas that come already wrapped up.

> *Out of the dun sedge*
> *of winter*
> *a snowdrop stands*
> *would that his cold heart*
> *could warm itself*
> *in some waiting flood*

Nowhere in my writings do I find myself as I know myself to be. And now I know I have been carrying the baggage of so many other people that when I put it down, I feel light enough to float away.

I have an almost superstitious feeling that against genetic odds I have been given a little more time to fulfill a task I set myself when I was very young. Had I said then, "You must write ten books before you die," I might now feel satisfied. Perhaps I would not feel as unfinished as I do now. But it never occurred to me that I might publish one book, let alone ten.

That is not how my mind worked. I did not confuse a particular objective, like writing a book, with my life's task. I could have said along with Kafka—whom I had not yet read—"I have a difficult task ahead of me and have dedicated my whole life to it. I do it joyfully and ask for nobody's pity. But because it is all I have, I ruthlessly suppress everything that might disturb me in carrying it out." How easy it was to try to identify myself with Augustine, Pascal, Kierkegaard, Proust, Kafka, Unamuno. But when I first had such thoughts I had read none of them.

Like everyone else I have spent most of my life earning a living, on the whole a meager one, and being responsible for other people. Throughout I never forgot where I began, with a basic intuition of selfhood. No matter where I was, I never forgot that intuition. It seemed to me so incredible that I should one day have to disappear. The question was how to clarify and use this fact wisely. Would I have enough time?

Now I am being goaded more than ever by the certainty that there is little time left. I know that it was this obsession with the shortness of time that branded me from the beginning. I did not need to read others to be convinced. It hit me unexpectedly in odd places and odd times. I knew that I had come from nothing and would go back to nothing. I knew my consciousness to be unique, with an unforeseeable life span. I fervently believed, with dread and with exhilaration, that the only thing worth being obsessed with would be a supreme effort to insert that certainty into everything I did. For sixty years that was the most consistent thing about me.

This is where I am now, renewing a passion that has never left me, my point of departure, time, devourer and challenger, my end, my beginning. With fearful concentration of feeling and reflection, body and spirit, I take up once more the worn ticket for my voyage through life. The ship may now be different; it may not be a ship at all, but a plane or a rocket. The passenger is not quite the same either, having, for one thing, more luggage to stow away. He can no longer be confident that he knows the geography of land and sea. He does not know whether it will be finite or infinite. All he can be sure of is that his part in it cannot be shared. That is, it is prudent to assume that he will have no companions. If he does, so much the better.

Half awake
his feet thread past sofa and chairs
mistaking moonlight on the lawn
for fallen snow
He has done this before
last night
the night before
and will tonight as well
Was it yesterday
or is it already tomorrow
and which tomorrow
someday
the last

We often say of other people that they act as if they thought they had all the time in the world. They are probably thinking the same about us. For years I was tormented at the end of each day, before going to sleep, as I reviewed what I had done that day. What had I done to justify my life that day, or had one more day, one more chance to live, slipped into oblivion along with all the other days? I could remember so little. I had wasted my life, and could not relive it. For I had accepted the proposition that since I could not recall what I had done, I could not possibly justify it. It was as if I no longer existed.

When I talked this way in front of others, they laughed or looked puzzled. Some were probably sorry for me. Why should anyone think he had to justify himself? Was it not enough just to exist? Was that not miraculous enough? Not for me. Unless I could be satisfied with the quality of my life, I could not think it worth living. I was not consoled by those who said that any living is better than no living. That seemed to me to miss the point. I was not concerned with a metaphysical question but with a practical question—what kind of life? And yet I believed, along with people who do know despair, that if one cannot think life worth living, one might as well not have been born.

My consciousness seemed to have been individuated from the start by an intuition of the self, unique and lying within an arbitrary parenthesis of time. I had not made myself, and I could not remember when I was made. I doubted that I would unmake myself either. The only question was what I could do with this parenthetical self. Time itself seemed quite neutral. It did not demand one course over another. I assumed my fate was to be erased at some moment, and after that it would be as if I had never been at all. I could not hold this thought in my mind longer than a second or two, it was so horrible, so incredible.

I had been given—and I knew I was not alone in this—an unenviable vantage point. And yet it often seemed to me that it might be enviable after all. I was the privileged center of my awareness of the world. How could anyone else feel like this? From this isolated view I could see all the other islands, but I could not see the world as they could. When my island disappeared, a privileged view would also disappear.

As a pastor I had seen how quickly friends and relations are forgotten. Few of us live for long in the minds of others. Into the ground, then away from the cemetery to the waiting cars and the drinks somewhere. Besides, after many years we know that this world will someday itself cease to be, and with it people, memories, libraries and their books.

How strange that each of us has a uniqueness, his own life, his own awareness, and that it is here right now, in America, not somewhere else in time, not in the future, not in Africa or Asia. This is the most fundamental fact that each of us has to deal with. And so it is ironic that anyone should suppose that he has plenty of time.

When I say to myself that I ought to be seeking a time that is mine alone, that will satisfy my need to make something of myself that no one else can, I am not thinking of a length of time. Good time has no length. Bad times certainly do; they go on and on. A good time may be very short, as measured by a clock, or very long, but we do not notice that it is long, absorbed as we are in whatever we are doing. We learn very early in life that we can lose time and waste time. At best we become unaware of time as we enjoy what we are doing.

Most of the time we look at ourselves in the same way we look at everything else, as if from the outside. We also know that we will be alive still after others die, and we know that when we die everyone else will still be alive, with more people on the way. Most people have never heard of us, and we have not heard of them. Anonymity is a condition of our existence.

The awareness that is behind the writing of this page is privileged, aware both of itself and of what is outside it. No one else has this privilege to know what it is like to be oneself, and I do not know what it is like to be someone else. Sometimes I think I do, but I really do not. We know ahead of time that the privilege is going to be withdrawn one day. In exasperation we ask, "Why should I have been given this chance if it is going to be taken away?"

27

Some will say that it is a waste of time to think such thoughts. True, there is nothing we can do to save body or mind, and most of us do not believe anything will. And yet it is not at all a waste of time to wonder at least whether there may not be a way we can be true to the privilege of living, a way to justify a singular destiny.

There are times when we lose someone we care for, and cannot take in the fact that the one who was so alive is now dead. It may be easier to feel the enormity of the loss of another person than the prospect of our own death. Most of the time the enormity of anyone's death eludes us.

It bothered him
that sometimes
his intensity
left no room
to breathe

What can we do to justify our lives? How will we know when we have? I cannot depend wholly on the assurances of others that I have made it. They do not know the depth of my longing for justification. I am not comforted by the well-meant assurance of those who like me enough to give me credit for doing my best even when I have not done anything I myself consider special. Anonymity is real enough, but recognition, even when not spurious, does not remove my own demand that I find proof that I have uncovered my secret self. Naturally, no one else thinks of that as a problem.

If success, length of life, recognition, are not what I am looking for, what then is important? Why should I be asking the question now? Why does it linger so insistently? Could this be one of those quasi-metaphysical questions that are unanswerable? I do not think so.

Some questions cannot be answered if they are taken out of context. In this case, the context is all the aspects of the secret self, not just its shortness of time. As I see it, had I known more about the other aspects of the secret self earlier, and not just the urgency that comes from the shortness of time, I should not be asking the same question about justification over and over.

Overwhelmed by the basic intuition of the self, I was diverted from acknowledging the full content of the intuition by the temptation to succeed like everyone else. I should have paid more attention to certain attendant aspects of individuation. I have always known them, but in my habit of mentioning them in the context of other people's ideas, I had not given myself time to see them in relationship to each other. This represents the kind of delay in understanding myself that I see as characteristic of my life of reflection.

There is a limit to the welcome we ought to give to recognition by other people, just as there is a limit to the time we should spend on their opinions. I say this only because I have given so much of my life to reading and listening, and do not fear the accusation of being locked up inside my own opinions and ideas. But we cannot know what is worth approval until we have found out by ourselves what we are meant to be.

We say we are sorry for some people because we believe, even if they do not, that they are meant to be more than they are. And yet who can tell what anyone else has had to put up with? Even the closing in of death does not scare some of us as much as the intransigence of obstacles massed before worldly success, or even the perennial conflicts of family life. We cannot expect everyone to have the stamina or the courage to refuse to let adversity smother the self.

There are, we know, people whose determination, whose single-mindedness, strikes others as ruthless and selfish. But they are not made any differently from us. What separates us is the impact of their sense of self. It does not take much to discourage the development of an interior life. In America, at least, the interior life is regarded as marginal anyway. A flash of vision of the self, once and perhaps never again.

It is impossible to know how many people experience such an inner vision even once, let alone several times throughout life. Perhaps the intense resolution that even the most extroverted show has as an inner motive a half-forgotten memory of an intuition of self.

Such a resolve sets one person apart from another, and also marks the lives of the most ambitious among us. Anyone who feels quiet gathering around in the twilight of life may be a person who once had an intense vision of himself early in life.

There is a fine line
I cannot draw
between the ache of longing
and the ache of loss

The vision of the self, its acceptance of the urgency of its need to see itself as a whole, appears in various forms. At the most general, it is endemic restlessness. I myself think of it as the mark of the human. In both Latin and French there is only one word for restlessness and disquietude. "Cor nostrum inquietum est . . . " (Augustine): "Condition de l'homme: inquiétude" (Pascal).

I think of restlessness as the more general of the two, and more physical. Disquietude suggests an interior unease. But I do not insist on the difference. In my case, disquietude can lead to restlessness, and if not dealt with quickly, may deepen into depression or despair. I do not suppose that there is anyone who has not been restless at some time, and many are restless all the time. Restlessness is a symptom of life: disquietude is perhaps optional, as an interior life is optional.

For many there is no end to restlessness. The attainment of one objective is superseded by a trek toward another. That, at least, is a way of looking at both restlessness and disquietude. Another way is to see them as dissatisfaction with any achievement that does not match ultimate desire. This is how Augustine thought of disquietude (or restlessness), and his understanding is typical of the religious mind.

I do not believe that what the religious mind says it wants is radically different from what the nonreligious mind wants. For both, the paradigmatic sentence I have already quoted applies: "I was looking for you long before I knew you existed." The only question is which pronoun makes more sense: "You" or "you."

I have never believed that the quest is everything and the goal unimportant. That would let one off the hook. Nor do I think that motion is inferior to rest. We may want rest, but motion is the way of life.

Nor do I think that the voyage of life should be understood as a return to a mythical paradise, or to a mythical or essential self. There are those who do, and they are respectable minds. My own working assumption is that myth can suggest but is not normative. What each of us needs most is a self that is ours alone, not a Platonic copy of a Platonic idea. I have come to see more clearly than I ever did that the voyage of the self is a haphazard journey from port to port, land to land, that I have probably visited before, but which I was not prepared to call home. It is as if I were tracing a figure in the sand, making the lines clearer and deeper all the time until finally there could be no misconception of what I was trying to show.

The yearning
that he spent on God
and his Mother
bounced back empty
when he heard
the hollow voices
of their mystery

It might be thought after what I have just said that I have always felt as strongly as I now do about the primary urgency. I have not. The intensity has increased until it now sometimes threatens to suffocate me.

What I like to call disquietude because it sounds more serious than restlessness, I once took to be a symptom of a self looking for God, insatiable without God. When I stopped thinking about God, when, in fact, my existential thinking became more concrete and descriptive, I realized that I would have to change my terms in order to minimize my dissatisfaction with theology. At that point my disquietude felt like nostalgia, homesickness for a home I might have heard of but had not yet found. As a child I had never been away from home, and had never known homesickness. I knew my metaphysical nostalgia would have to be looked at more carefully. It felt like a lovesickness, except that it lasted far longer than any frustrated love.

I have always been attracted to *The Castle*, where the cynical Amalia tells the naive K. that it is probably not the Castle that he wants to see but the charwoman up there. Was it God or was it a woman that I really wanted? I didn't know.

I was equally moved by the writings of the women mystics, seeing more in their yearning than I could see in the poems of secular lovers. The intensity and the persistence of their loving exceeded anything I had come across in books or real life. Because they expressed their love of God in sexual terms, I wondered why they had not looked harder for some human being to love. Or had they done so and been rejected? Was God a last resort?

The intensity of their passion and the pattern of their lives were models I would retain all my life to measure longing by. Gradually, however, I came to acknowledge that I did not have their talent for the intangible. And yet in a curious way the mystics often made it look as if their intangible love affairs with God had become tangible. That seemed to me to be a delusion, and I was never tempted to try to follow them. I knew that would lead me to despair.

Camus said that nostalgia is the mark of the human. I liked him for that. The trouble was that he did not mean by nostalgia what I did. His nostalgia was philosophical, even political, abstract rather than earthy (except in "Return to Tipasa"). He wanted justice, meaning, unity. I wanted places and persons. Later I understood why. He was a young man when he wrote that. Life has a way of curing one of abstractions, no matter how noble. The sensuousness of life that should be so natural for the young, and which they often take for granted, can mean more in later years when one fears he will be deprived of it. I myself share with Kierkegaard a strong distaste for abstraction, and always have. It is about all that is left of my sympathy for that wounded man. Philosophy has always seemed to me more unreal than mysticism or poetry and fiction.

By the time I was in my twenties I had become very sure that I would never be at home anywhere but in the visible world, and only with minds that were as impatient as mine with the abstract. Fields, trees, hills, the sea, the sky I would not care to trade for Plato or Aquinas. What the theologians in their superior way call "created being" was all I wanted. Like Cathy Earnshaw in *Wuthering Heights* I knew I should feel desperately lonely if I were taken away from places I loved. And at this time I began to associate created being with human creation, particularly painting and music. But I have never been tempted to think of art as a substitute for religion. I had learned about passion from religion, and I would never be able to feel as passionate about the arts. For me they were not to be compared to people and places.

By now
it might be thought
he had earned tranquillity
instead
each morning
he fought a battle
between longing and despair

Long after I had stopped taking nostalgia as a guide, I began to transfer my inner determination to an even simpler and more persistent sentiment: longing. Perhaps that had been the underlying feeling all along. I may have been misled by my reading into giving it different names. Or was it more personal than that? I finally realized that I must live with a desiring that has no built-in end or promise.

It is somewhat difficult today to trace the way restlessness became nostalgia and nostalgia became longing. For a long time I was not aware of any change taking place. For so long I had used restlessness, disquietude, nostalgia, longing interchangeably, as if they were phases of the same phenomenon. For a while I even added insecurity—I fancied the Latin *insecuritas*. That was when I was professionally and financially insecure. But I meant the word to cover more than that. It was also at a time when I was thinking more about anonymity and recognition than I now do. One after the other I saw the pertinence of each of these words diminish, and today I am left with the only one that has outlived the others, longing.

I have been thinking here of a kind of spectrum of restlessness that might match a spectrum of darkness, from boredom to demoralization. I can see this more clearly today than in the years when I was so preoccupied with insecurity. I do not claim any privileged acquaintance with the dark emotions. It was easy for me to draw on my own limited failures and discouragements to imagine the worst. Because I knew I had done nothing much to justify my life, it was relatively easy to imagine a range of shadows in the interior life. Now that I am more or less secure and have done almost everything I ever wanted to do, I feel nearer real depression than before. It does not make much sense, except as a symptom of a purification of longing, the longing of a repressed secret self. I have reached the extremes of both desire and missing out.

I have learned ways to keep darkness at arms' length. A disciplined mind has many resources to call on. It can shut out darkness by keeping busy. It can explain away desires that have failed. There is, however, one desire that cannot be explained away, and that is the desire to follow the calling of the secret self. If I were now to try to suppress all longing, I should have to suppress the very foundation of my soul.

Sometimes longing can be but a sign of the self marking time, waiting for definition, or waiting until it is free to be itself. Sometimes it is as if we had been waiting for a crisis to tear us apart so that there is nothing left but the secret self. I may be close to that now. I may be experiencing a revival of my original intuition, with the added knowledge that I have not done enough to take care of it. Now that I no longer have to make a living, I have time to throw the dice one last time. I admit there is something risky in thinking that way, for if I fail now I shall have no other occupation to fall back on to distract myself.

Sometimes he was forced to say
such and such is bad
when what he really wanted
was to say
look how lovely

If there is a central theme in my writing, it is the theme of restlessness. I ask whether I am more restless than others. Probably not. But my preoccupation with restlessness has had a puzzling feature. I have never been quite sure why it is so important to me.

When I look back to my childhood, I recall that I was more physically active and more imaginative than the boys I played with. I was not surprised that my parents called me high-strung. And I knew it was a criticism. I gradually learned to avoid their displeasure by holding myself in, and trying to be a model of self-control.

Later when I was told by others that I am impulsive, I was surprised. And only when I was made to understand that that was not meant to be a criticism did it occur to me that both impulsiveness and restlessness might just be a blind side of a suppressed self trying to get free.

I then remembered that when I was called high-strung, it was on occasions when I was feeling especially good, and when my high spirits seemed to get on my parents' nerves. What was gaiety to me was lack of self-control to them.

Now that I am beginning to understand the motive behind the restlessness, I can see how much I have deliberately prevented myself from feeling. I had tried so hard, in filial obedience, to give my parents no excuse to criticize that I suppressed spontaneity and even joy. Anyone who could look at snapshots of me as a child and then as an adult would be struck by the transformation from an open to a closed face. It is a wonder that a sense of humor has survived.

I can now interpret certain episodes with more under-standing. Although I have always looked forward to vaca-tions in the Greek islands, my most memorable vacation was spent in Africa, in Burundi, where for two weeks I was for the first time able to lay aside responsibilities. Even though I was suffering from angina at the time, I felt more alive there than anywhere else. The world seemed com-pletely new, and I felt as if I was one of the first to see it. I know now that Africa has had this effect on many others.

A year later, when I was recovering from a coronary bypass, I underwent a manic phase that troubled those who saw me. When I joked, "I want to join the Foreign Legion," I was trying to convey how wonderful it was to be alive and full of energy again. But the uneasiness of family and doc-tors came through to me as a repetition of my parents' dis-pleasure when I let my spirits soar.

I have blamed my philosophical bias for repressing the imaginative side of me, I now see for the first time that this was only a symptom of a deeper disorder which my preoc-cupation with the several forms of restlessness has until now never understood. I cannot interpret the restlessness of other people, but I know my own restlessness was my psy-che's way of telling me that all will not be well as long as I continue to hold back spontaneity.

> *There was a time*
> *when he said an antiphon*
> *at mass*
> *to the God who gave joy to his youth*
> *and a time when he would sing an antiphon*
> *to a Titan Venus*
> *his life, his sweetness, and his hope*

Before writing this essay, I had two constraints in mind. I promised myself that I would not use quotations or refer to books. I wanted what I had to say to stand on its own. Second, I had no idea of writing an autobiography, partly because I do not like to talk about myself, and partly because I do not think my life interesting. I have now broken both pledges.

I realize that it would be unnatural to mention certain themes and not acknowledge that I know how other people have used them. I also realize that I should not hesitate to mention some things that I have done, without which much of what I want to say might seem artificial.

Stendhal, as I have said, wondered what he was. So have I. But I do no longer. What difference does it make whether I call myself a poet or a philosopher? Strictly speaking, I am neither. Isn't it enough to say, "I think and I write?"

Probably I should say more. When I look back over the years, particularly at some of the places where I have lived, it is obvious that I remember less of what I read there and how much I enjoyed being there. It is also true that my intellectual life was nurtured in and by New England and England, Harvard and Oxford. Both have, at least in winter, inhospitable climates. Perhaps intellectuality and cold weather go together. In fact, as a person I have been more solitary than most.

And yet by the time I arrived in Oxford I had read myself out for the time being. I now recall little of what I read at that time. I remember sculling on the river, long walks and bicycle rides. Above all, I remember my exposure for the first time to brilliant and witty conversationalists. I listened carefully, and thought about what I heard.

The turning point came, without my realizing it at the time, while I was at Fribourg for a semester and took a week off in May to visit Howard Schomer, a Harvard classmate, in Florence. For the first time since my spring vacations in Charleston as a child, I was transformed by the warmth and loveliness of the South. Both spontaneity and joy returned, for a week. I went back to Florence and Fiesole during the next two summers and, after leaving Oxford, lived for a year in Greece where I was married. By that time I had been inoculated for life by something more than intellectuality, even if the inoculation did not seem to have taken for a long time afterwards. I now see that these two opposing climates match two sides of my being.

I have led a life that has required constant reading. And yet a substratum of my mind has been sustained by memories of the bells of Oxford, Fribourg, and Florence, the cypresses of Fiesole, the pines of Attica, and the stony, herb-scented hillsides of the Cyclades. These actualities, as much as all my reading, writing, and teaching, made me the person I now am. That is why I responded so emotionally to Africa when I most needed its warmth and color. I remained, nevertheless, a cat that walks by itself.

He passed a chain gang
in the South
when he was a child
they stared at him
as he went by
now we all live
in chains we ourselves
have put on
and only once a year
walk unchained
let us weep
for Cinderellas

Had I been like others who have little time for an interior life, I might have been given useful clues to my lost or hidden self through dreams. But longing has done for me what night-dreams do for many others. There is sometimes a moment in life, if one is lucky, when we say, "Just a little more and I will understand at last something I have been waiting for all my life." But the moment comes and goes, and we understand nothing special. I know other people sometimes say that they find what they need in their dreams. In my case, I would have become more disheartened had I looked to my dreams for help. As it is, I was for a long time tempted by Augustine to wonder whether I had not been looking for happiness in the wrong place or in the wrong way. That passionate North African was able to convince himself that what he had been looking for all over the place was all the time waiting quietly inside him to be released. For my part, I could not be persuaded that by abandoning the world I would be left with anything but illusions.

For a long time I could not progress beyond the acknowledgment that longing was near the center of my total awareness of reality. Only recently have I understood that longing is one of the elements of the secret self.

I have up to now avoided the word *passion*, not just in my writings, but in my conversation. Feuerbach called passion "the hallmark of existence." My upbringing has made me wary of overcharged words. I do not want to sound emotional. But I think I always knew at some level of consciousness that I was passionate by nature. Why not admit that Feuerbach was right? If a mystic can confess her passion for God, what is wrong with a nonmystic confessing a passion for the creation? A time comes when one has to forget some of the constraints that other people have imposed.

I think I never completely abandoned hope that even if my nostalgia had no home that it longed for, even if my disquietude had not led me yet to God, I might still find it possible to look for a credible complement for my longing. I had passed my life believing and not believing, or, more accurately, trying to believe and failing, looking here and seeking there, giving up and finally not giving up.

I had identified myself, in rapid succession, with the passion of mystics and poets, novelists and even some philosophers, never finding one whose life and explanations of life convinced me for long. I never lost the conviction that I was born to see, if not to meet, something or someone that could complete my soul.

I was as time-driven as ever, all the more so as time became shorter. I was frustrated in my inner being, and yet determined as only an impatient and impulsive man can be who has seen his goal slipping farther and farther off. At this point I woke up one day—I cannot remember the day—to realize something I had never admitted before: I was lonely. And it was a loneliness that had nothing to do with other people, or so I thought.

You led my very soul
so lightly through the days
until there was no more room within
then cried me on
until I could no further go
alone

When I say "loneliness," I have in mind that separateness that is at the heart of each individual and that when intensely felt can be an inspiring demon to challenge each one to face the almost incredible shortness of his allotted time. Augustine called it "a great solitude." It is out of this loneliness and because of it that essential solitude is born. Indeed, to think about oneself is an exercise in the relief of radical loneliness. What purports to be a mind at ease with itself as it talks about itself is in fact a mind that before speaking understands that if it does not speak it will suffocate. The most powerful autobiographies are privileged confidences that few of us are worthy of. Autobiographies charged with the intensity of near total revelation should be reserved for times in one's life when one knows how difficult it is to tell the truth.

If we look too closely at our inner selves, we can be struck blind by our torments, so stunned that we cannot recall the very particularity of the self. Get too close to anything and all is a blur. But if you can imagine or invent a self something like your own, as in a novel, you may come closer to knowing your own life. That is why it is easier for someone else to tell us that which is vividly true about ourselves which we might go a lifetime without noticing. Friends can sometimes tell us what we are incapable of telling ourselves, even unflattering truths. But it takes a sympathy that is in some way parallel to us to look past the barriers we have spent a lifetime trying to raise.

For some there is place enough
and even time
for others neither time
nor place
for him it seems
a time and place
to see the flower shake
and feel the warm earth tremble

I am astonished as I look back at the very great diversity of people I have known, many of them well known in this country and abroad, particularly artists and intellectuals of all sorts. As a teacher, pastor, and traveler, I have met almost every kind of human being imaginable. I have observed and listened well, and acquired a perspective on human diversity that has made it impossible to take myself too seriously. I have lived in several different parts of the United States, and have studied and traveled in Europe, Africa, and Asia. I have not lived in isolation from my fellows. I have a close family and good friends. When I am restless or unhappy, it does not occur to me to find relief by seeking out people. I make no connection between my moods and the presence or absence of others. And so when I say I am lonely, I do not mean I have lacked companionship. What I have in mind is a more complicated state of being, a compound of the essential solitariness of mortal man, and a kind of suspension of life as I wait for something or someone to complete me.

Our minds usually do not hold more than one idea or sentiment at a time. It is hard to keep two in suspension for long. One of them tends to overweigh or overshadow the other. So it is not surprising that I never considered passion, longing, loneliness in a fixed order. Had my sense of urgency been seen closely related to longing and passion, and had they in turn seemed related to loneliness, I should not now feel frustrated as I try to see myself as both an individual and as a whole. I should have been able to see that somehow I had not experienced the most basic acceptance and understanding that a person with my intense feeling and passion for life wants.

I do not now doubt that there was also a perfectly obvious reason why I played down loneliness. I feared I could do nothing about it. My youthful adoration of the Blessed Virgin (the feminine principle of the universe), my yearning for intimacy, for nonjudgmental acceptance, had been put aside when I felt my longing unreciprocated.

It is a mystery to me why one person's empirical sense is more highly developed than another's. I myself never needed any instruction from Hume or Kant. I knew what I wanted, and I knew the limits of what I could believe. Nowhere did I find a two-way encounter that could satisfy for long. I did not find more than I desired or deserved. In truth, I did not find much of anything. I should prefer to be telling a different story.

Whoever says that he or she wants to be understood and accepted is not looking for something abstract. That is why the Christian insistence on the importance of persons makes sense. Christianity is not about theological abstractions or their formulas. There is one book in the Bible that does not mention God at all, *Song of Songs*, that speaks of nothing but human longing and human satisfaction in images that are recognizable to everyone. No wonder that its songs are so seldom read in church. The mystics loved this book, because they found it a model for seeking, finding, losing, adoring. To be accepted as the person one wants to be, that is its dream. But who is good enough for that? Who is strong enough to give the dream to anyone else without losing himself or herself along the way? The mystics answered, "Only God." Therefore, God?

Must we conclude, can we conclude that because we seek, therefore we will find? It takes courage to turn your face against this. We know how hard it is for most people to admit that anyone can die in vain. Why should we also stubbornly assume that since we are alone at birth, we will not be just as alone when we die? Some religions do promise acceptance and understanding, but to most people their promises seem intangible.

Who can be satisfied with longing alone? Is it not wrong to encourage longing if we cannot guarantee satisfaction? Is not that precisely what we accuse the mystics of doing? Their fantasies are very impressive, but they only underline their human loneliness. What is the good of losing one's hold on the real for the sake of a dream, no matter how beautiful?

Is this the worst that can happen? Possibly it would be even worse if we were to be granted our wishes, if longing were to be fulfilled by means of another human being, and then we were to lose that person. That happens. Or even, if one fantasizes like John of the Cross, one might think that God has withdrawn. What is the difference between believing that God has withdrawn and losing belief in God altogether? A dark night is lonely, however you look at it.

Desolation feels the same no matter how you care to interpret it. Is it better or worse to fail to meet the person you long for or to meet that person and then lose him or her? What an impossible choice! What a possibility! If one never finds any satisfaction, are we supposed to say we are not meant to? Either way we feel cheated.

Have I just made a case for suppressing longing? Is the nonintrospective person right after all? Why dwell on such things since there is no hope of ultimate satisfaction? I am not yet ready to accept defeat, even though I have seen some of the risks. The risks are nothing compared to the need.

It is daybreak
and I feel
hollowed out
as if front and back
have caved in

When I returned to Oxford, an old friend, Vincent Turner, with whom I had lost touch in the interval, looked at me and said, "Life seems to have treated you well." I was astonished; I had thought of myself as someone just hanging on by the toes, as I used to dream when I was recovering from a childhood sickness. It then occurred to me that those I was accustomed to think of as successful and happy might, like me, feel different inside. We seldom know how others really feel; so much of life is covered over by putting a good face on things.

We all have dark moments and more than we know live from one dark moment to another. The twentieth century has destroyed more men, women, and children than any other. Spiritual changes too have affected even the most comfortable. And yet I fancy that at the beginning of the century many, like my own parents, were relatively indifferent to darkness and evil. They seemed to live in cocoons. If they ever felt any deep uneasiness, I was unaware of it. Words like *depression* (except economic) and *panic* were not in their vocabulary.

My own strategy has been to acknowledge openly the limitations of the voyage of the self, the impossibility of getting off safely once embarked, the chance that pirates might attack or some plague strike. But at the heart of the secret self there is always a specter of having someday to admit that one did not know where he was going, or that one could not get there, if he did know. It is easy to understand the attractiveness of diversions and distractions.

We set rules for survival, and accept rules others persuade us are good for us. The more successfully we seem to make do, the less we notice our secret selves and any hopeless longing.

But is it so hopeless to wish to know the shape of each self? Is it hopeless to think that what each person needs cannot be found? I have never been willing to accept that. I do not believe in the absurd, as Camus said he did, and I do not accept absolute insecurity either, like a character called Pascal in one of Marcel's plays.

Why not? Because I believe there is some empirical hope that we need not go so far. No one ever told me that I have a secret self. I found that out by myself. I shall have to find out for myself how the self's secrecy can be satisfied.

> *In the morning*
> *he lay on one side*
> *looking through the parted curtain*
> *at the spruce trees*
> *and planned the rest of his life*

I have spent part of my professional life trying to say what the existential theologians and philosophers have not said clearly enough to suit me. I sometimes felt as if I were doing their work all over. And sometimes I even wondered whether they knew what they meant as well as I did. They certainly did not write as plainly. I felt that they, too, might have learned from having to teach a course in freshman English, as I did. Only Unamuno seemed to say exactly what he meant. When I was nineteen I learned from him much about the conflicts and passions of life and mind.

We are obliged to live by rules laid down for us, shunning introspection and working hard for recognition. In America, failure is the evil most of us fear most. As the years went by I saw others succeeding while I seemed to stand still. It was only slightly consoling to hear of those who had got to the top and then collapsed. They seemed to have found success irrelevant to something unspoken inside them. Could it be, I wondered, that an instinct, undeveloped or suppressed, of a different kind of self, a secret self, had finally stepped in and said, "Give up, you have wasted your life on what does not matter"?

Few become successful who have not known what it is to be restless. What one does with restlessness determines whether one takes the primary or secondary road. If you see restlessness as a goad to success, you may miss the primary need, to become fully conscious of your secret self. Life does not always give one a second chance.

Most successful people seem to be satisfied with themselves. By the middle of life it is too risky to speculate much on one's course. The successful person whose self-image collapses may still be an exception. And yet how many there are who talk to therapists just to keep going from day to day. Few can look naked terror in the face, and what is more naked or more terrible than a self that doubts its course?

It may be prudent to acknowledge unease, as prudent as a patient who has learned not to conceal pain by too much medication. It is better to know whether the disease is still there. And prudence demands acknowledgment of longing as well as of pain. The question is, longing for what?

I may have made it look as if life is made up of conscious decisions, like working out the proportion of attention to the secret self and attention to worldly success. It is not like that at all. So much time is spent just idling, at best waiting for something to happen. We seize on the most trivial of unexpected arrivals, events, letters, phone calls, to justify taking our time or taking time out. We miss the point. Waiting for a Godot is a waste of time. He is not going to come.

*All his life
he had waited
to feel alive*

The person who waits for someone he did not know existed is in better shape than one who just waits, thinking that waiting itself is hopeful. Not many can say of themselves that they are waiting for the day or the hour when all will be revealed. That would signify the existence of a deep passion that few people today are sophisticated enough to believe in.

Those who wait have told themselves that there will be time, always time. Even when they cease to believe this, habit sometimes keeps belief alive. Still time? And if one says, "No, there is no time left, not for you anyway," the fire in the self sends up smoke signals. "Who knows?" it says.

The agony goes on. Would it make any difference if there really were time? What could we be told, what could we find, who will then appear, what will we understand that might make the quality of life deeply satisfying?

It seems to me now that such questions miss the point. They temporize, and all the while time is running out. In effect, they waste time almost as much as the fanaticisms that vitiate so much of the intellectual and political life of our time. Sometimes I think that it must have been a lot easier to face oneself fifty or sixty years ago. I am forgetting for a moment the weight of suffering and hate in my life-time. Must we know our secret selves only when we are about to be wiped out?

What makes many of us so desperately anxious to avoid anonymity, and what leads us to look for places where we will be kept safe and warm, is not so much that we know we can be lost as that we have a deep fear of not being able to remember the secret self.

We are always being misled by well-meaning friends and relations, and by the self-assurance of the successful among us. What works for them should work for us. For that matter, even philosophers and theologians mislead, the first by telling us what cannot be, and the second by telling us what should be. The authority of parents is hardest to escape. If we believe them, we are misled. If we do not, we are forever haunted by the suspicion that we should have believed them. How the spark of autonomy each of us has can stand up to them determines the amount of time we will waste. In order just to survive, we have to learn to take authority lightly. There are enough real conflicts around without having to gnaw on the mistakes of our parents all our lives.

Today an increasing number of people try to relieve tension through some kind of meditation. But if one medi-tates only to empty the mind of tension and fatigue, the unfinished business of life will have to be dealt with in other ways and at another time. The traditional methods and theories of meditation in both West and East treat detachment as only preliminary to a consideration of the central questions of the relation of self to the real.

Anyone who has ever asked friends at the dinner table what they would like to have been if given a chance to start all over knows how unsatisfactory most answers are. People suggest ridiculous or improbable things, and not always very different from what they are already doing. A better question is, what can I do that I have not already done? What am I really meant to be? That is the kind of question that may get a more plausible answer, like, "On the whole I should like to be more of what I am just beginning to be." Or, "Do I still have time?"

When I talk this way to myself, I find encouragement to travel back to my point of departure. I should like to be able to answer my own questions. I am not willing to take the raincheck represented by the Zen prescription of "sitting quietly, doing nothing." In fact, I feel as if that has been precisely what I have been doing—nothing.

I know the rules, I know the players and the games. I have come to the point where it would be a waste of time to keep looking for what I have found many times over and thoroughly examined. I cannot expect any surprise wisdom now. I am long past the point where it makes any sense to envy the complacency of others. They have got where they are by bypassing much of what I know to be true. I cannot now fall back on some plot or theory as a substitute for my story.

At daybreak
a band of lemon
at sunset
a band of apricot
snowwhite all day long

By this time my mind had become sleepless, without even the chance of a dream to show me the way. I confess it would be a relief if it were not so. But relief is not what I am looking for. I am looking for pointers from the secret self, and I have a hunch that I may still find some.

So much of anyone's life is arranged for him or her and then rearranged. If it were not so, there would be no stability, and most of us have more stability than we realize. I believe in stability and in equilibrium. I even believe that we need a certain quantity of sameness from day to day. We cannot survive emotionally if we are always being challenged by something new, and always having to adjust to the flickering of circumstances and inner turbulence. We would not be able to carry what we learned the day before yesterday into tomorrow. We would have no reserve of judgment or understanding to apply to what we cannot always be sure is different or the same.

We can count on the seasons, and once in a while, even on the weather. We live by circadian rhythms. We have artificial routines each day also, familiar jobs and jokes, faces we know at home and on television. We do not want to have to give much thought to everything that appears before us; that would be unbearably boring. We know there are vicarious, harmless ways to keep boredom at bay without paying any price beyond the cost of a book or the electricity to run the TV. No one should have to argue in favor of security. All most of us ask is to be spared unpleasant surprises, and no more than our share of pain.

We like to know what we can expect of others, and they of us. We appreciate consistency and the keeping of promises. There are great advantages in being the kind of person who, unlike Henry Adams, does not "always expect the worst, and finds it worse than expected."[5] We can put up with sameness to escape that. We have worked out just what we can put up with, and what we require others to put up with from us. Most of us are junior masters of accommodation.

I do not disapprove of accommodation in itself, only when it interferes with recollection of the needs of the secret self. Seldom do friends and relations surprise us. That is the way we like them to be. And yet the reason for this is that most of the time all of us are living outside ourselves, by routine, arrangement, accommodation, in short by suppression of individuality; and yet that is a mark, even when out of control, of the human. We do not like to be reminded that the only sure test of a free mind is its capacity to do something it has not done before. We prefer to dismiss freedom as fickleness and irresponsibility, so that we will not be distracted from our own assumptions of what is worth paying attention to. Emotionally speaking, there is much to be said for predictable people. We know before they open their mouths what will come out. They are safe, and through them so are we.

The secret self, however, does not worship sameness and predictability. Out of the essential urgency and loneliness, it longs for what it does not yet have. It may for a long while not know what that might be, and so it lives by the pattern contained in the line, "I was looking for you long before I knew you existed." That *you* may be imagined to be God, or it may be supposed to be another human being. So far as the longing is concerned, it makes no difference. That is an emotional question, not a reality question. It is the first question that the secret self asks, and many answer it without going on to raise the second question.

There is a well-known popular notion that says it does not matter what you find so long as you are satisfied with it. Feeling is all. That is not much worse than recommending, as Pascal did, that we act as if we believe. I have only rarely seen evidence that one way of life or another results from believing anything, or from acting as if one believed. And yet belief of any kind purports to say something about reality. But does it?

Those who pray hope for the unexpected, or they would not pray. When they say that they are looking for grace, they mean that they are looking for a gift they have no right to expect. Prayer cannot manipulate reality. What it does is signify some trust in the nearness of mercy. In that respect, it is probably better to pray than not to pray. At least, an important feature of the real is attested to, even if nothing comes of prayer. This is, I suppose, an elementary metaphysical point. Prayer must also mean, if there is any point to it, that the person praying does not shut himself off from grace, in other words, from the unexpected.

He awoke
one morning
inside a box of light
all white and gold

I would say more. Whether in prayer or through conviction about the nature of the real, I must acknowledge that the secret self does not have its own answer. In other words, introspection is one thing, introversion another. One does not go round and round the mulberry bush of the self for ultimate satisfaction. That would be sick. Longing has to find its complement outside itself, if at all. It is only in despair that it is even understandable that anyone should turn in on himself. That leads to narcissism, and is a far cry from the role of the secret self, as I am thinking of it. God, or another person, but never self on self.

We speak often of seeking this or that, even more generally, of seeking the kind of answer that would speak to our individual longing. But this is a seeking that does not find; it is a seeking that hopes to be given, hopes for grace, hopes for an unforeseen present of life. Everything that I have already written elsewhere about presence speaks to this point.

The Platonic image of the two halves of the whole round self seeking each other and not being satisfied until once more joined, is an edifying and lovely myth. But there is no reason to think that these halves were ever one round ball. The most that the myth suggests that we can accept is that we seek some kind of completion through another human being. The question is, what kind?

I doubt that most of us really know what kind until it is almost too late. Time does not seem to be on anyone's side where this is concerned. Only afterwards can one say, "Time was good to me." Reality beyond us has its own schedule and its own plot. This is why it is common to speak of luck or chance. It takes an irrepressibly religious mind to hold that there is more to it than that.

The most secret of secrets is that we do not know what we need any more than we know whether what we need will be given. But if and when the time comes—a good time it will be—and we are given what we need to complete ourselves, then it will be tempting to suppose that reality has a deep reserve out of which the gift of presence can come. Believe this, if you care to; it makes little difference to the outcome.

A much surer truth is that the secret self is a deep reserve out of which a decision may arise to acknowledge the gift or let it pass. In either event, the self will be secret no more. It will have fulfilled its function, to present itself to the world for completion.

If he did not know
this soft air
and golden light
could be April or October
when desire and fear
chase each other
around the table

There is a parable in Kafka's *The Castle* that suggests the way of grace and the unexpected. A man goes to an official in the middle of the night for help. Only that official can help him, and if the man catches him at the right moment the official will give him the help he needs. But the man in the story is fast asleep when the story is being told to him, and does not, of course, get what he had come looking for. So with grace. It has to be seized when offered. It is meant for each of us and for no other. We will not be given a second chance the next day, and maybe never. At least, that is what Kafka felt.

Who can complete another self? Certainly not one who wants to remake someone else in his own image, but only one whose presence, whose understanding and encouragement make a person feel more himself than he ever imagined he could feel. If the first thing we know about the secret self is that it is an autonomous secret, the second is that to be really alive one must be acknowledged by another self that is equally autonomous. This is exactly what one looks to God for, perhaps because most of us cannot believe there exists any other person powerful enough to do the same.

Perhaps this is what is behind the line in *Song of Songs,* "Love is strong as death." Death is not to be feared once the secret self gives up its secrecy, its reserve, and is accepted for what it is. This is the most that reality has to offer, so why linger? The worst that one has to fear is missing the unexpected when it comes, or not really understanding that it is meant for us. This is another thing Kafka understood: there is no general grace, only grace for me and grace for you, at this time and at no other.

Something more has to be said. There is more than individual salvation at stake, more than the bringing of the secret self into the light of day and out of the darkness of its reserve. In abandoning secrecy one opens oneself to everything else that can be experienced in this world. Just as secrecy was once a barrier between persons, now there is nothing, in theory, between the completed self and everything else. This is what it means to experience immediacy— nothing left between us and the world. This is only possible once the self has been released from the obsession with its finiteness. I believe this takes place only when the deepest needs of our being find parallels in the vision of life of another person. Perhaps this is a way of thinking of the human being as an image of God.

It is not in the power of anyone to make himself really happy. It is only in his power to prepare himself to be understood and accepted. But first he must prepare himself by observing the conditions of selfhood: finite time, mortality, urgency, aloneness, longing, and above all the impossibility of satisfying longing without acceptance. Since this cannot be counted on, one must also be prepared to dream of the unexpected. This is what the mystics and all other poets of mystery have done. So when and if the gift of reality comes, it comes not just from a specific source but from the very nature of the real. Amazingly this encourages men and women to surpass themselves in another way, by creating new actualities that strike observers as also having a deep reserve. The deepest art comes from secret selves that have come to know themselves, in spite of their secrecy, as wholes. This is what is meant by individuation.

There is nothing to fear when secret selves meet; they need lose none of their independence or individuality. All they lose is isolation and secrecy. They have gained the wholeness that they were looking for. We are most alive when we are willing to be accepted.

The philosopher and the theologian call this presence. The philosopher sometimes speaks of immediacy as well, an aspect of presence. The theologian speaks of grace, unexpected giving and undeserved receiving. Both the philosopher and the theologian believe that there are special experiences in which some independent reality may confront us and give us a chance to be what we are meant to be. Each of us will know what that is when it happens. Then the suppressed self will arise out of its hidden reserve into the open space where secrecy is no longer needed.

The ideal should be to be able to see things as a young child or as primitive men and women, with no barriers between the imagination and the world of living presences.

The high point in a life would not be seen within the secret self but at the place where the whole person feels free for the first time to reach out without fear of being put down. Reality may look quite different from then on. It would be as if a cloud were lifted, confusion blown away by a sudden wind. Everything would be clear at last. It is also as if a purification of the soul had taken place. We would say at such a time that this is what life is meant to be like: wonderful, miraculous. How absurd to have lived so long and have almost missed out altogether. This is what it means to feel alive.

All his life
he had wanted
to feel at home

When I was a student, I lived in Micklem Hall, the eighteenth-century annex of Campion Hall (designed by Lutyens in the thirties). When I returned, I was assigned a guest room just across the landing from my old room, and was informed that my room had been turned into an oratory. When I looked in, I saw that they had removed bed, chest of drawers, table, and chairs. It was empty except for a large Greek ikon of Mother and Child on the wall where my bed had been.

On my last evening, after Evensong at Christ Church, I looked in once again and found a Mass in progress. The Jesuit Master of Campion Hall was sitting cross-legged, like a Zen master, on a cushion under the ikon, discussing the Epistle and Gospel for the day. I felt that I had come home.

It was a reconciling moment. And yet I knew that I had not come back to a room or a liturgy that would be mine in the future. But it was the kind of home that one can return to for wisdom and fortitude. The voyage would still be hard and lonely, and yet I now felt that it was one I would be sharing with others. Perhaps that is how Augustine felt after a while. I had had to discover it for myself.

For many years I have been haunted by a parable ascribed (by Benjamin Fondane) to Kafka. "You are being reserved for a Great Monday."—"That's fine, but Sunday will never end." This is how I had felt until that moment back in my old room. It was then Sunday, and I knew that Sunday was almost over and that a real Monday would soon follow, the Monday of my return to America. Since then I have been assured that I was more right than I knew; there is a Great Monday after all.

I have not said
the last word
yet
not tomorrow
not next week
not ever

About three months later the announcement of the Louisville Grawemeyer Award in Religion for my book *On Presence* changed everything. It brought me a sense of achievement that I had never known before. In the weeks between hearing of the book award and a long-planned vacation on the island of Patmos, something strange happened. I seemed to lose touch with a part of myself that I had felt sure of. I had been so accustomed to a solitary intellectual life without recognition that I was thrown off balance when recognition came. The importance of the unexpected had been one of my favorite theories for years, and I now discovered its power over me. I was so unprepared for it that overnight I seemed to change character. The initial surprise and pleasure were succeeded by a feeling of vindication that I had never had a chance to feel before, and which, I am embarrassed to confess, I openly expressed. I had been more or less anonymous for so long that I soon began to feel uncertain about my apparent success. For the first time I understood how Rilke could imagine the Prodigal Son rejecting the gestures of love shown him when he returned home. I had wanted recognition, for my persistence if nothing else, and when it came I did not know how to handle it with modesty. By the time we reached Patmos, I was ashamed of myself, and began to doubt whether I deserved anything at all. The new confidence I had brought back from my Oxford visit was gone, and I doubted myself more than ever.

The mourning dove he mistook
for an owl
was calling its mate
from the bougainvillea

When I was first married in 1940, we lived in Greece for a year. Since then we have returned to Greece many times, usually to the Cyclades, and three times before this year to Patmos. I have looked forward each time to cloudless summers, clear dry air, and bright blue seas. I have always felt more alive in Greece than anywhere else. I used to say it was a model for the landscape of paradise. This year, however, it took much longer to adjust to paradise. The soft air made me so lethargic that I did not want to walk at all. Only after a week of lying around, feeling as if I were recovering from a long illness, did I begin walking slowly up the hill from the port to the monastery and village encircling it. By the beginning of the third week I felt strong enough for the long rough walk along the shore and over the hill shoulders to one of the most beautiful sand beaches in the Aegean.

I had gone to Patmos confused, at the very time when I should have felt good about life. Instead of delight, I felt a distaste with my own character. Perhaps that, more than the fatigues of writing, made me so lethargic on arrival. But just as strange, one morning I awoke to find the lethargy and the confusion lifted, leaving a tranquillity that was new. For the first time in my life I felt there was nothing more to worry about, that I could not be touched by self-doubt or anger ever again. Something had been worked out for me under the surface of my mind and feelings, and I felt myself to be whole and safe. In a sense, I was empty, empty of bad feelings, but more than that, quite free. Could this, I said to myself, be the beginning of a Great Monday?

A rooster crows in the dark
before dawn
the sky reddens
and church bells madly ring
like train bells at a station

Kafka's parable of the Great Monday gives no hint of the kind of day that might be. The implication is that one may never know, for Sunday will not end. It is a parable of thwarted vision, blocked hope. I had not needed Kafka to believe life is like that. And I do not recall ever wondering what a Great Monday would be like.

When I wrote about my secret self, I thought that the best I could hope for would be acceptance and understanding, and maybe a little encouragement. Now I began to wonder whether there might be something beyond that, something that I might be on the point of experiencing. I had arrived in Greece, seemingly having forgotten my moment of reconciliation in Oxford, feeling more incomplete than ever. And that was because I had been thrown off balance by unexpected good news. I had finally been assured that I was not a failure, no longer anonymous.

George Steiner's *Real Presences* concludes with the curious suggestion that Saturday is the longest day, and that the day of resurrection, Sunday, follows. For me, and for many Christians, it is Sunday that seems interminable. I should like to think that there are at least hints of resurrection in the midst of the interminableness of Sunday, when one is waiting for a new week to erase boredom. Unfortunately, I have always felt too close to Kafka's pessimism to make this live. For me, as for many Christians, the day of resurrection was often a day of tedium, not joy. Like the Great Monday, Sunday, the day of resurrection had never really come.

Of course, I have known light as well as darkness, and yet something had prevented me from assuming that the traditional explanations of the Christian Year made sense of life as I lived it. I think that is in part why I had to wait so long for my awakening on Patmos.

Churches shut their portals
when he approached
the righteous turned their backs

Seven years ago I spent ten days wandering among the twenty monasteries on Mount Athos.[6] I was taken in as a guest in all of them, but made to feel a heretic in some. I had wanted so badly to be accepted. Why else should I have traveled so far to be there? I even thought I might be considered enough of a Christian as an Anglican to be welcomed as a brother Christian. When I was rejected, even after my protests, which for pure comedy should have been good enough to get me in, I felt so unsettled that I began to ask myself where I did belong. Something in me, some lingering sentimentality about religion, then began to harden.

On my previous visits to Patmos I had always visited the great monastery that dominates the island, visually and historically. I treasured the memories of standing on its roof and gazing out over the Aegean as young monks, with habits flying in the wind, tugged the bells for services. This summer I looked into the courtyard once and backed away. I felt the time had passed when the life of this or any monastery had anything for me.

For much longer I had backed away from using the words *spiritual* and *spirituality*, and I felt uncomfortable whenever I saw them used easily, if not casually, by those who have no traditional religious affiliations. I continued to associate these words with the mystical traditions of Christianity, Judaism, and Buddhism, and the distance widened between the practice of these traditions and my own life, even though I continued to read the same books that I believed had nourished me in the past.

This year I had not gone to Patmos because it was a holy island, as Greeks call Mount Athos "The Holy Island." Even though I reread *The Book of Revelation* before leaving home, my chief interest in going once more to Patmos was to spend three tranquil weeks on a quintessential Aegean island that had not yet been ruined by tourism.

The sacred grotto
in the pine-covered hillside
once a cave open to sea and sky
now shut in by stones and mortar

John the Theologian (not John the Evangelist), who wrote Revelation, had been exiled by the Romans from churches in Asia Minor, just out of sight to the east of the island. The grotto is now called the Cave of the Apocalypse because when he lived in it he heard voices and had visions of the future of mankind. This book has been a model for apocalyptic writing and modern prophecy. Anyone familiar with the symbolism of Old Testament prophecies and apocalypses might think of John as a plagiarist and dismiss him as unoriginal. Perhaps his plagiarism is ignored not only because most of us no longer know his sources, but also because of the tone of personal conviction and horror that dominates the book as a whole.

What struck me most this time was that I could not understand how he could have sat there looking out over the sea and other islands and not at least have mentioned the view. Had he sat with his back to the view, or was the inner vision of doom so intense that he did not notice? I knew that had he lived in the sixteenth century, in Italy or Spain, instead of in the first century of the Christian era he could not have avoided the outward as well as the inward view. I thought of a similar scene from a poem of John of the Cross, and wished John the Theologian had not been for some reason prevented from recording what he too could see, as in: "My beloved is the mountains / the wooded valleys and sequestered / the strange and distant islands / the loud resounding rivers / the loving breezes with their gentle whispers / the still and tranquil night / as it kindles with the coming dawn."[7]

As I sat on the stone parapet outside the Cave of the Apocalypse, the gentle breezes were just as loving as in John of the Cross's Andalusia. Here too the tamarisks, oleanders, olives, pines, and aromatic shrubs enhanced one's appreciation of the gift of life. But for several centuries in the Christian era the old classical feeling for landscape had been lost, returned to civilization only during the Renaissance.

Each time I sat on that low wall I thought of the fondness John of the Cross displayed for caves that opened up on panoramas, as did the novelist Stendhal. They both liked to retire to caves for solitude and for the refreshment that framed views can provide.

Indeed, there is another kind of cave, too—the interior cave of dreams and turbulence that inhibits the growth of the spirit, just as the outer world of television, anger, and politics today obscures the interior life. The greatness of John the Theologian was not so much that he foresaw Armageddons as that he forcefully stated his belief in a Great Monday when there will be no more mourning or sadness, no tears, but rather a New Creation.

This was his vision of The Second Chance. And it was on Patmos that it occurred to me for the first time that there might be something beyond the sense of reconciliation that I had felt in Oxford.

Sailing along the coast
in a caique
welcomed
by the aromatic perfume
in the hot air
from the spiny clumps
on the headland

Here was a paradox I was not prepared for. I had known life to be a continuum of good and evil, of inescapable as well as avoidable experiences of all sorts. I was very proud to have read and seen and understood so much. I thought I was civilized. If anyone had suggested that sometimes all this might be put aside even for a little while, I would have thought him ignorant. What sense would it make to forget all I had worked so hard to learn?

And yet there on Patmos, at the end of a long life of worrying over the best and the worst history offers, I seemed to be waking to a new intuition about life, that I was for the first time really on my own and free. Free at last!

I am not so naive as to depreciate either achieved or received wisdom. And I feel reasonably certain that I would not now be able to see anything clearly had I not worked so hard to understand things rightly. But wisdom had finally become an external burden, and I needed to put it down for a while.

On Patmos I experienced a merging of self and my surroundings that I had occasionally glimpsed before but immediately lost. I had wondered whether it is possible to describe what it feels like to be alive, that short, sharp, and yet warm sense of surrounded self, so simple and yet so elusive. And as I gazed beyond the balcony outlined in bougainvillea, I caught the fragrance of early morning in Greece. I exclaimed, "Greece again!" And then, "This is what it is to be alive." Later in the morning as I walked by myself along the shore and again smelled that mixture of oregano and some nameless herb, I said, "I am part of all this."

How simple minded, this sensuous connection. But I felt it, breathed it, loved it. And I was convinced that until each of us finds himself at one with the natural world, he lives in a jail of isolation where even his connections with other people lack an important dimension.

Is this what spiritual directors had in mind when they counseled methods of dispelling distractions to prayer? And yet their counsels were complacently embedded in assumptions that are alien to me now, the existence of God and the chasm between this world and another. Should we not try to put such thoughts in brackets and say only what we know from experience? Can we not start from the beginning and learn to see? Real spirituality does not come cheap. It is not an additive or an inheritance, but, if real, a product of natural sight. We cannot ride on the backs of the saints.

I agreed with Rilke that "it is possible that one has not yet seen anything real or important." I felt as if I was seeing something both real and important for the first time. I had lived with the second-hand, with hearsay, too long. Almost everything that filled my mind to the brim was vicarious knowledge. No one can go home to Ithaca for us, not even wily Odysseus. Each of us has his own journey to record.

Once again he climbed the hill
once again he stood by the stone corral
once again he looked down at the sandy
beach
once again he had won the right to look
at paradise

The vision of Psilli Ammos seemed to me a vision of paradise. There was Artemis in the distance, Artemis of the Patmians. There, too, was Actaeon watching her from behind a tamarisk. I myself had seen her naked but had not yet been torn into pieces. The altar stone in the monastery had come from her temple, as John the Theologian had come from Ephesus, her Asian shrine. She had sailed to Patmos long before him in order to immortalize herself for us.

Buber said that one does not find God either by staying in the world or by leaving the world. Perhaps not. But I am quite sure that I will never find anything very important by leaving the world. On Patmos I had discovered that even the worst contradictions of life can fade. The day I learned that was one of the most important of my life.

When I stood on the ridge looking down at the sand beach, the tamarisks and lines of surf, I no longer saw it as distant, an unattainable paradise. I felt as if there was no empty space, no separation between me standing up there and the figures below. Air is not empty either, but freighted with elements we do not see. I, the air, the sand, the sea belonged together, as flesh belongs to bones.

Now I look out of my floor to ceiling windows in Maryland, over my herb garden and over the cornfield to the woods beyond. All is lush and green, as Patmos was dry and rocky. Again I feel, not just know, that to be alive is first of all to be enveloped by nature, and that I am privileged to be able to feel and say it.

On Patmos I understood something else that I had only tentatively thought in the past. I remember an impassioned digression one evening in one of my classes, when I found myself insisting that there are two kinds of people, those who are so shut up inside themselves that they seem to have no interior life at all, and those who are always trying to get out of themselves somehow. I tried to find the right words and failed. But in my embarrassment I used the word *spirit*.

On Patmos I realized that all my life I had been thinking about spiritual matters, especially the interior life, the elements of which I have spelled out here. My intellectual journey—my spiritual journey—had taken me to many places of the mind until it became absolutely clear that my central theme has always been Presence. Whether when thinking about Sophocles or Dostoevsky, Proust or John of the Cross, I had always been looking for clues to the intimacy of self with reality. I had long since given up drawing absolute lines between religious and nonreligious, spirit and flesh. It was existential, living knowledge that I had been trying to understand all along. But my central passion to see and say what I saw left me less and less satisfied with what others told me I should see.

> *A beach of pebbles*
> *and dry white seaweed*
> *a distant goat bell*
> *the gentle lapping*
> *lapping of the waves*

Just as it is true that we cannot go home again, so also it is true that we are seldom given second chances. And when we are, they may be inhibited by recollections of failure. We miss opportunities we later regret. So much of anyone's life is sodden with burdens from the past. It is hard to see or do anything fresh.

Now when I think about Patmos, I think of an entirely different kind of second chance. When the torments and confusions of the mind subside and for the first time we feel that they are not going to return, we begin to think of the future as an extended present. The first hint of this for me was feeling the unity of myself and nature. I now believe that this is a precondition of the life of the spirit.

I know that *spiritual* and *spirituality* are words that mean little or nothing to many people today. And until now I myself have avoided using them either in speaking or writing. It is not easy to find convincing analogies between our experience and interpretations of experience that one finds in books. I do not know for sure whether my new understanding of spirituality has much in common with traditional usage, although I am certain I have not been unaffected by the latter.

I should like to feel that my new understanding of spirituality does have something in common with some of those men and women whom I have always thought of as masters of the spiritual life: Augustine, Eckhart, Pascal, John of the Cross, Teresa of Avila. I have always felt I had more in common with them than with most of my contemporaries. And yet I have also felt that their way could not be mine. For unlike them I do not take God for granted.

Spirituality does not come from thinking about God. It comes from having an active interior life, one that is constantly aware of its incompleteness. That is why longing—nostalgia, disquietude—is so important. Longing separates spirit from matter. But longing becomes both desperate and shallow if it is not grounded in listening.

Not everyone has an interior life, and consequently not everyone lives in the spirit. Of course, everyone thinks about himself or herself, reflects on feelings and problems. But there is a good deal more to the interior life than that. Spirit is a way of standing back, waiting, looking for new experiences that make us feel more alive and more useful. My outline of the secret self is only a preliminary description of the need each human being has to reach out for, accept completeness, and offer the new self to the world. There is a Michelangelo drawing of Christ rising from the tomb[8]—gliding, soaring—that is for me an exciting model for the life of the spirit, not self-enclosed but expanding. To escape from imprisoning desires and worries and feel not only safe but free, that is what it means to be spiritual. Many live without knowing this.

An interior life is a prerequisite for spirituality, but it is only that, a foundation for a life of presence, that is, total giving and receiving, mutuality. In the presence of another person we feel we are on the way to being complete.

Beyond the beach grass
over the salt flat
up the twisting ravine
to the city on the hill

On Patmos there is a half-moon beach in a bay called Grikóu, quite desolate even at high noon, where morning after morning I liked to sit undisturbed on the dry white seaweed and gray pebbles. Before me across the channel there is an uninhabited island in the shape of a camel, and often the faint sound of a goat bell. Behind me and almost out of sight the great fortress monastery skirted by a white town. Grikóu is very quiet, except for the lapping of the waves. I went there to consider my newfound peace.

Grikóu became an emblem for a third and final stage in my understanding of spirituality, much like the prayer of quiet in which, for a few, the soul knows that God is there, but for others "the word God seems to mean nothing."[9]

I had discovered something in my experience that I had been told only advanced religious know, the quiet of "secret contemplation."[10] My own experience was not in the dark, as was St. John of the Cross's, but met in full sun. Only by stretching language could I make any connection with John of the Cross's two famous nights, the night of the senses in which there are no satisfactions in praying, and the dark night of the soul in which the soul feels it has lost God altogether. After years of trying to compare my own sense of reality to John of the Cross's, I had reluctantly given up. It seemed to me more likely that the most theology in our time can honestly say is that God, if there is God at all, is indemonstrable and unnameable. This used to be called negative theology. I had stopped calling it anything. What was left was just a pattern of an experience that, underneath the theological jargon, John of the Cross and I might yet have in common. I found encouragement for this view in reading his poems.

The quiet of Grikóu was not the quiet that Proust speaks of, the quiet that settles around us as we grow older—although I was beginning to find that real enough—but the quiet that accompanies the draining away of all striving and all fear. Nor was this quite the same as a purifying of distractions that the masters of prayer write about. This was more a quiet of something finally achieved.

The quiet of Grikóu confirmed something I had wanted to believe, that spiritual experience has to be understood descriptively, not theologically. Spiritual states do not need formulas and hypotheses to be identified by. It makes little difference whether one calls it the peace of Grikóu or the prayer of quiet. Nothing much is added by imagining God hovering over everything. For me, Thomas Aquinas' metaphor for the motions of contemplation stays closer to what

I experience: the circular, the straight, the elliptical or spiral. They are suggestive rather than interpretative.

I am in no position to judge the reality of other people's experience, or their interpretations. All I can say is that they are in no better position to interpret what I know first-hand. Nevertheless, when I admit that I have felt I had something in common with some of the mystics, I also feel when they speak of God in ways that set up a space between God and the self a desolation throughout my whole being. Only when they speak of the incompleteness of each of us in our life's struggles do I feel in communion with them. When I read them, as when I read Alain-Fournier's *Le Grand Meaulnes*, I am reminded of much of what I have here called "The Secret Self."

Another way to say this is to say that it was as if I had been told of things that very distant forebears experienced in an utterly different kind of world than the one we live in, and in spite of the vast differences between them and us, I felt a curious affinity, a silent, restless yearning for whatever might yet complete my soul.

So now I have reached the stage where I seem to have discovered a Great Monday. And I can see that so far as I can understand the meaning of my own descriptions, that Monday is not unlike much of what John of the Cross, Teresa of Avila, Mechthild of Magdeburg, and Ignatius Loyola took for real. Ascending Mount Carmel seemed to have much in common with a Great Monday. And now I say, if it feels the same, who is to say it is not the same? To say, as John of the Cross did, that in the dark night the soul loses its awareness of God's presence and yet that is when God is more present than ever, may be true. But how could he or anyone else know that? What we can say for sure is that for John of the Cross at such a time, and for me at Grikóu, a good place had been discovered, a place where one could find some peace at last. He called it infused contemplation. I call it confidence.

In the gap between the pines
the sun had already set
someone now brushes the sky
with waning apricot and rose

I do not have to leave home now to find a Great Monday. As I sit in the middle of my living room, picture windows to the east and picture windows to the west, quiet rules the center for a while. John the Theologian, too, could have seen the sun rising in the east, as I do. He seemed to have seen nothing but the troubles he had left behind in Asia in the seven churches, and the coming day of wrath. How intensely he looked for vindication. Almost as an after-thought, it seemed to me, did he recall the promise of the first resurrection to ordain a second chance for mankind.

At Grikóu I sat facing an East in which I had seen a sun rise over the hill across the harbor in Skala. And I had fol-lowed that sun back to the United States, no longer fearing the night. I had discovered some real boundaries in my life, and concluded that all was well after all.

I believe that the center of the interior life, its spiritual-ity, is yearning. Leave that out of your life, and you become a one-dimensional being, one that will curl back on itself if not released from the bondage of self-regard. But if it dis-covers the power of presences, real, not imaginary or intel-lectual, it may proceed to a third stage of the spirit, the experience of quiet.

I have been stressing my familiarity with John of the Cross because, unlike his friend Teresa of Avila whose uncontrolled imagination, however entertaining, can get in one's way, John was like many of us who refuse to be shut away from the natural world. In his most personal effort to describe the life of the spirit, he wrote the kind of poetry that I for one should like to be able to write. And if he had not been importuned by pious nuns who could not feel or think for themselves, he would have seen no need to say, "This is what I mean." What he meant is what he said, just as what *Song of Songs* says is what it, too, means.

The opening stanzas of "The Spiritual Canticle" could be the epigraph for "The Secret Self," especially its nostalgia. "Where have you hidden away / beloved, and left me here to mourn? / having wounded me you fled / like the hart; I followed on / behind you, crying out, calling—and you were gone / shepherds, you who wander / there by sheepfolds to the mountain height / if you should chance to see / the one I most desire / tell him I'm sick, I suffer, and I die."

A breeze moves the bell
suspended from the hawthorn
the lilies sway in tandem
never again will he feel alone

Spirituality's center is always an affirmation of some presence. It is empowerment, healing, life. John of the Cross's eleventh stanza sets the goal for the whole canticle and for our future. "Reveal your presence to me / and kill me with the sight of you, your beauty, / for see how nothing heals / love's sickness and its grief / except love's presence and the living being."

There is no mention of God or Christ in this poem, or in *Song of Songs*. Is one more spiritual than the other? I cannot see that it is. No wonder that my contemporaries do not know what to say about *Song of Songs*, and John's contemporaries did not know what to say about "A Spiritual Canticle." Most of us like formulas that do our feeling and thinking for us. And when we make use of them we confess that our understanding of the spirit is second-hand at best. I go further and say, worse than second-hand, arrogant.

Near the end of his poem John describes a quiet that is similar to the quiet I felt on the shore of Grikóu. "There you will reveal / that which my soul had sought for me on the way, / then you will give me / you, my very life / that which you gave me the other day / the breathing of the air / the nightingale's sweet song, the glade / its grace and splendor, / in the silent night, with flame / that burns away yet brings no pain." Why ask for more? Is there more?

In truth, probably not much. For the Great Monday has begun. Nothing good, nothing lived through to the end, has to be renounced. All that is needed is the triple recognition of yearning, presence, and quiet. Each of us can have his own experience of this triple crown, as I did this year in Oxford and on Patmos.

All day long
in the dry still heat
the cocks reveled
in the pines
and cicadas sang
along the cypress walk

Once before I had felt this quiet, the summers of 1938 and 1939 when I stayed at the Villa San Girolamo in Fiesole. I remember sitting morning and afternoon at the end of a cypress allée and looking down at the city of Florence and its Duomo in the valley of the Arno. I was not a convalescent like the other residents, including my two companions, a young Scottish Dominican friar and an American painter. I did not even need a rest after my desultory studies at Oxford. I tried to do a little writing, which came to nothing. And yet I entered a period of contentment, both undeserved and barely appreciated. To call it a foretaste of Patmos is literally true, but that would be to brush over the difference. It was a quiet of suspended life, not the quiet after either ecstasy or turmoil.

What I found on Patmos was more complicated than contentment. It was a kind of time-release of the elements of presence: astonishment, gratitude, understanding, confidence, and an opening of the whole self to the future. The more I have thought about this, the more I realize that these are always present when one is recognized and accepted by others. To liken the peace at Fiesole to the peace at Grikóu would not only fail to take into account the differences between a young man and an old man, it would also fail to consider how much more complex and how much more radical the second experience is. I feel differently not only about others but about myself as well. At Fiesole I was living in a suspended quiet. Now I live strengthened to the point where I feel a strength and serenity that had always eluded me.

The quiet of Fiesole was an isolated experience, not to be encountered again for a long time. It said little about the quality of my life then. When I felt something like it on Patmos, it was after a long, full, and troubled life that had culminated in a final clearing away of fears and conflicts beyond expectation. Something like this is said to take place within the mystic way. But there are many kinds of quiet, so how can one be sure mine is like another's? I recognize in mine a mixture of purification, astonishment, confidence that contemplatives are also said to know, and a mingling of individual persistence and sheer chance.

This is the quiet that puts the seal of approval on the experience of presence. When one person is truly present to another, the atmosphere of mystery surrounding them is still. At this point in life the past can no longer hurt, and is no longer needed as a model. Not that existence is timeless, rather, the line between present and future blurs. I am trying to record only what I know, not what I have read, and I know now more than I ever anticipated.

In a dark night
my house being quite still
I saw my soul rising
from my body
hovering and complete

That day I had been talking to a friend about spirit as presence. In the middle of the night I got up and wandered for a while around the darkened house, conscious but not wholly awake. For the first time in my life I had a sort of vision, a glimpse of my own soul, round, opalescent, floating just above my head, yet tethered still to my body. All that day I had been talking passionately, breathlessly, about the openness of the spirit of man, of spirit as presence, of spirituality, of the ages of spirit and openness in the West.

That night my vision reflected all this and convinced me that as human beings open without reservation to all that is real and all that is possible, they bring themselves to the completion that has always been implicit in what we know of humanity. This is what I had been looking for all along, from those moments in childhood when my secret self had resolved that before I die I should define myself. That very day I had been trying once more to say what I believed, and perhaps as a result of the effort had, as it were, forced my very soul to be exposed in all nakedness.

During the next day I began to understand that the contentment I had found in Fiesole when I was a student had even less to do with my new sense of peace than I had supposed. The quiet was deeper because it was something achieved by the inner struggles of my life, all the visions and revisions, the failures and the persistence. For the first time I saw that my future could be a seamless extension of my present.

At this point, whether that day or another I do not now remember, I had a second vision, less physical than the first, but no less indelible. I felt enveloped in and part of a world infinitely larger than my own. For the first time in my life I felt that without ceasing to be myself I was surrounded by the whole. It was a moment of deep mystery and sobriety, and I felt at home. I knew that I had been on the right track all along as I traveled through a landscape of doubt and anxiety, not satisfied until I was assured of a fitting end to longing. Far from being frightened by sensing the enormity of the whole of reality, I felt reassured that at last I had found the horizon of my longing.

And so I will order my days to keep in mind what I have learned. I shall not forget the journey just because I can now see where I have been going. But as the old distractions fade, I want to try to compose the rest of my life so that I can hear the wonderful sounds of silence.[11]

C   O   D   A

Fribourg Spring[*]

He could see the snow-covered mountains of the Bernese Oberland as he stood at the lectern reading pages of Aquinas on contemplation. Always ready to be distracted by the scenes outside the window, the Berne-Lausanne expresses that ran through the cutting below, or the mountains in the distance over the city.

Late one November afternoon he had taken the first local leaving Oxford, one car and an engine on the run to Fairford, and got off a few miles up the line at Yarnton. It seems that Newman had once been seen, long after his conversion, walking in the night outside his former church and vicarage at Littlemore. And so he too, having made a decision that would change his life, wanted in advance to establish a place and time to remember it by. The little walk that evening through the ground mist between Yarnton Halt and Cassington would be the beginning of a lifetime of moving about, as it turned out, to Fribourg, to Paris, Sils Maria, Fiesole, Innsbruck, the Greek Islands, Cyprus, Cairo, Capetown, Copenhagen, an expanding rosary of place-names he would invoke for his spiritual exercises.

When he stood at the lectern in his room at the Foyer St. Justin, he had no idea that he was already tied to an

*From *Queen's Quarterly* 921 (Spring 1985): 157-61. Reprinted by permission

inner wheel that had begun moving long before in his child-hood and that would never stop until he died. An inner restlessness that he had been endowed with could not be given away or erased. By the time he came to Fribourg he knew what Augustine and Pascal had said about disqui-etude; he had read about Barth's *insecuritas* and Heidegger's *Sorge*. He knew the names of the "boundary situations" of Jaspers. No one of his generation had read more, or could more accurately identify the faces of *Existenz* in Dostoevsky, Nietzsche, Kafka, and Proust. And fifty years later the pho-tographic negative of his studies would still be developing inside the acid of his perennial musings. At the end of each day he had had the habit of asking, "What have I thought today that justifies my life?"—as if life can ever be justified by thought. Each day as he earned his living, he tried to exercise his little gift for defining and refining the terms and structures of the interior life. He had learned what it is to get off to a running start and then stall. He had learned what it is to be cleft by contradictions between desire and frustration, between dreams and shoddy performance. Yet he never said, "It was a mistake. I should not have taken the train to Yarnton."

In the spring of 1938 life should have been idyllic, in that walled city, with Gothic streets and fountains, ramparts and city portals. It was a place of baroque churches and a small Gothic cathedral with a famous organ, on the bank of a deep winding river spanned by suspension bridges. At its small university students, friars and wandering scholars from all over the world sat on tiered wooden benches, like bleachers, hearing white-habited Dominicans explicate in Latin Catholic philosophy and theology, and thumping on the wooden floors when their lectures amused them. The streets, as in medieval times, were spattered with the white, black and brown of religious orders. In the afternoons he walked into the showery spring countryside outside the city walls, pausing at isolated shrines guarded by sleepy mastiffs, opening doors of darkened convent chapels, kneeling to pray. No Heloise for his Abelard, he was only a spectator of the past. But he would not forget the place-names. Bourguillon, Perolles, Gotteron, Morat, Maigrauge. And as cement takes time to set, his own mind slowly set as he daily exercised his passion for visual beauty, meditating the while in some austerity on the shapes of his imagination.

Later in life he would be tempted to say that other people have no inwardness. It would be a waste of time, for he learned how hard it is to draw a line between his habitual musing over feeling and memory, and the commemorative pictures of occasional breakthroughs. Each man is a *grande profundum*, some deeper, some greater. For each the interior life is a burrowing and a burning, in silence and solitude. We are always wanting to reach out to find something—or someone—new, always longing, constantly failing. We are homesick for what we have never had or even known. It is a condition of exile from a paradise we can neither remember nor describe.

An inner life means resigning oneself to instability, to being unsatisfactory to oneself and unfinished. It is also at bottom romantic, even erotic, in all its fibers. We are questions with no answers guaranteed. What answers there are may be right for others, but only encouragement for ourselves to try again. An inner life is like a pressure plate holding back an awful force. Its disquietude is nostalgic; it seems convinced that life has a point and a purpose, but is ignorant of what the point is. And so lives are condemned to endless striving for an end.

Even so, the interior life of man is more than *insecuritas*. It is more than quiet musing or despairing exploration, more than melancholy and self-pity, more than a sensitivity to the passing of time. These states only define the beginning of understanding that *samsara* is teleological, and that the real end is still to come. The clutch can be released, a sense of purpose sought for and an identity confirmed. Reasons can always be found for doing anything, even the thing that is right for one in the end.

We learn that one choosing excludes many others, that conflicts and impasses result from a way taken instead of a way not taken, or more confusingly, ways that other and wiser people have taken. Out of dilemmas a new disquietude may be born, and grow up to be despair. What looked so right can turn out to be a kind of hell. One does not always find fault with the reason or the way to hell, only the necessity. Self-pity is a shadow cast over the name of tragedy, and lingers because it is plain that one cannot go either forward or back. The inner eros has a hidden end, death. Nevertheless, eros must not be repudiated, for without it there is no life, only a waiting to live. And tragedy, which seems to be a last point of finitude, brought about by one's own choice, is the place at which the hero forgets heroism and accepts an opportunity to be a human being, and only that.

Springtime in Fribourg, 1938, the war a year away, the Nazis figures in Swiss students' humor. One could not foresee the death and misery of so many, or even the fate of private excursions that would never again be comforted by romantic dreams of a harbor of churches. He had thought it possible to pass from restlessness and longing to the peace of a believer, just by kneeling and praying. Had not Pascal advised it? Like better minds than his, Barth's and Jaspers', he had thought he could move from the first stage of Kierkegaardian inwardness to the third without getting hung up on the second. He just did not know enough of life to understand the intransigence of its logic. Cheap grace is always hard to resist.

He learned also that boundary situations are not *dei ex machina*, and do not open the gates of grace. They only lead to the question, "What shall I do with my life?" Only much later, after floundering and false starts, does one become ready for final questions, like "Is this all there is?" or "Can there be a second chance?" All the answers one has catalogued and taught speak not of "the truth that is true for me," but the truths that were true for someone else. The action of grace is not of the same order of truths that reason is at ease with. For grace plays in particular times and places, for and through particular people. Grace is something felt, not something thought, something accepted, not something chosen. Grace has no fancy ceremonies like religion. And even ceremonies are made plausible only by the intensity of desire, the complexity of the imagination, and the juxtaposition of inwardness and circumstances.

Whoever thinks that he knows the true shape of inwardness should be told that civilized man has always claimed to know the inwardness of God as well. Every theology is a kind of kabbala, someone's inner glory. And the shape of the interior life as it is actually experienced, seems not very different from traditions of the secret life of God. Both begin by contracting and withdrawing a pace (*Tsimtsum*), breaking vessels and scattering sparks, and in a period of undetermined exile waiting intently for a return to paradise, a restoration (*Tikkun*) of wholeness. Would it not be wonderful if Saint Augustine and Meister Eckhart and Isaac Luria were all correct in believing that the mystery of man's inner life is a true mirror of the dialectic of God? How consoling, how infinitely pathetic, are the ways of intellectual exaltation!

Such learned thoughts were withheld from him in 1938 when he joined the noonday promenade down the Rue des Alpes, scattering *saluts* right and left to student friends, and when night fell and the moon rose above the ramparts joined them once more to serenade maidens enclosed in their private school on the hill. One asks too much of youth and ardor that it know enough, like Eckhart, to pray to God that he rid them of God. God would take care of that later, unasked. Or that the exiled sparks and presence (*Shekhinah*) should attempt to reverse Christ's famous leap to Earth, and by so doing return us to the desert of the Godhead. This heady talk ignores the sieges of imagined Edens where one would encounter mysteries no less finite, no less frail. "I am all at once what Christ is, since he is what I am." When finite matches finite, and perfection of striving coincides with individualized achievement, by chance, by grace, finite soul and self arrives at a place of infinite wisdom.

Even then the ultimate test is valid, "Is there something left undone, not yet felt or thought?" Propelled by eros and by ego, matured by now in obligations freely chosen, and tangled in the contradictions of their making, who does not at last deserve to hear. "You fool, you who thought all walls would tumble down before a ruthless seeker, listen now one last time!" And someone—or something—calls you by name, "Abraham! Eli! tolle, lege!" Now the music we wish we had composed can be heard, and the things we might have made can be seen, the paintings we would like to have painted appear; the world is ours at last. In fulfilled dreams and dramas the nightmares and the loneliness disappear, and a reprieve is allowed.

Fribourg in spring was a stage for such a drama, only the writer and script were not there. It seems that the inward journey, from romantic insight to analytic skill, would have to involve much grinding of gears and marking time. Sustained by invocations of place-name litanies: Charleston, Bujumbura, Fribourg—way stations along the chosen way—who does not weaken at times and wish that there might after all be a divine model for the heartaches and wasted days?

But where in the secret life of God are the bells of Fribourg and scents of Charleston that brought us joy, or the faces and voices of those we loved? Where the musing that accompanied desire? Where the resolutions and convictions?

In the summing up the last retreat, it is not some internal logic or simplicity that tells the story, or even the recollections of some success or other. Only an idealized conception of the inner life of God can be that pat and satisfactory. Our truth is made of separate little truths, like particular people and particular places, here today and gone tonight. Why should we even want to be relieved of all we had to be to arrive at where we are? It is wrong to believe that one is ever through with any part or station of our inwardness. That would only short-circuit life and make it drabber than it is already. What we truly are must feel like some suspended wonder, or kind of expectation.

Notes

1. Sherwood Anderson, *Winesburg, Ohio* (New York: Viking Press, 1966).
2. *Alien Spears* (Cambridge, Mass.: Samuel Marcus Press, 1937).
3. *Human Love: Existential and Mystical* (Baltimore: The Johns Hopkins Press, 1966), 117.
4. There is a longer version in his book, *Conversations with Isaiah Berlin* (New York: Scribner's, 1992), 25.
5. Letter to Henry Cabot Lodge, September 5, 1909.
6. *Journey from Paradise: Mount Athos and the Interior Life* (Baltimore: The Johns Hopkins University Press, 1987).
7. This and other translations from "The Spiritual Canticle" are by Lynda Nicholson in Gerald Brenan's *St. John of the Cross: His Life and Poetry* (Cambridge: Cambridge University Press, 1976).
8. Kenneth Clark, *The Nude* (Garden City, N.Y.: Doubleday, 1956), 398, fig. 246.
9. Dom John Chapman, *Spiritual Letters* (London: Sheed and Ward, 1937), 290.
10. *Commentary on The Dark Night, The Collected Works of St. John of the Cross* (Garden City, N.Y.: Doubleday, 1964), 318.
11. 1 Kings 19:2 (a literal translation of the Hebrew).